THE ART OF
CARIBBEAN BAKING COOKBOOK

A Recipe Collection Of Local Caribbean Breads, Cakes, Desserts And More

By Freda. Henry Gore

ISBN: 1984186124

ISBN 9781984186126

Printed on acid-free paper.

If you give any type of medical, legal or professional advice, you must also include a disclaimer. You can find examples of these online using your favorite search engine. Most professional websites that offer advice have these types of disclaimers.

2017

First Edition

I am the living bread that came down from heaven; he shall live forever

John 6: 51

Contents

Introduction: My story

Freda Gore is no stranger to the art of Caribbean Baking having grown up on the island of Dominica. In a family where she remembered everything that surrounded her parent's local bakery. When Freda was a girl the family bakery was her playground and she grew up making her own childish concoctions from leftover dough and cake batters. When most of her friends used their weekends and holidays to hang out with friends, she spent her time in the family business with her parents, helping to bush bread, greasing the cake pans, mixing the cake batters and grating coconut which would later be made into coconut drops and tarts. By the age of seven Freda was her father's shadow, trailing him as he catered and baked for local weddings, bazaars and church functions. As a teenager, the family relocated and moved the business to the neighboring island of Antigua. She continued working alongside her family in the bakery. Growing older and stronger she now helped in hand-mixing of flour and bun doughs, mixing batters for the rum cakes and making the coconut tarts, biscuits and breads. However, there were times when she felt cheated from the fun her friends were having since she was unable to go to parties, the beach or the local carnival celebration and at times she resented the business. And to make matter worse, some of her friends nicknamed her the "Flour Weevil". However, her family encouraged her and it seemed that Freda was destined to go into the family business and after high school graduation she attended the local hotel school, where she studied cooking and baking arts. Fate had its way with leading her in a different direction due to her early knowledge of baking and her academics. At the end of her 12 months training she was offered a scholarship by the local rotary club to attend the Cornell University school of Hospitality training. At the end of the training she was recruited by the school as their culinary arts instructor. A position she held for 15 years.

Freda continued her passion for baking and the cooking arts and on relocation to South Florida, she launched her Catering Service "Silver Palate Catering and Personal Chef Service", where she placed great emphasis in incorporating her local island ingredients into her menu planning. Now, as the tour host for Caribbean Culinary Tours, she traveled to different islands where you can find her scouting out the local farmers markets, bakeries or street vendors. "Writing this book has truly been a baking adventure for me and I am passionate about my Caribbean baking heritage" says Freda. International tourism has such a strong influence in the Caribbean and some of the local chefs are doing great things with incorporating other international ingredients to the locally grown foods. However, the art of authentic Caribbean baking will soon be lost if we don't preserve it for future generation. Chef Freda hopes that the result of writing "The Art of Caribbean Baking" will help to preserve the local baking recipes and culture of the Caribbean islands.

Thanks

Thanks to my wonderful family and friends who have made this book possible. Your patience has been truly a blessing; some of you have been my guinea pigs over the years through my trials, failures and successes. To you all I say Thank You! You are all my heroes.

Dedication

A dedication to Mr. Thomas C. Henry and Mrs. Ena D. Henry, who have both been my life mentors. Your love, patience and care will always be the catalyst that causes me to strive to be my best self. And as my angels now, I will always feel your breath and hear your voices guiding me forward.

Quick Breads

I am the Bread of Life.

John 6: 48

A Jamaican Folk Tale: "Go Man Go".

HOW MANGO GOT ITS NAME

A Jamaican friend shared this local folktale while running from his local slave owner. A slave got tired and stopped for rest under a tree loaded with fragrant yellow fruits. As he was sleeping one of the mangoes fell on his head and he heard a voice saying "Go man Go"; he immediately got up and resumed his plight. Later, it was stated that he named the fruit mango from the voice he heard saying Go Man Go" that saved his life.

Mango Avocado Bread

Mango and avocado are a very seasonal fruit in the Caribbean. They are both in season during the summer months so combine them in this unique tropical-tasting and moist bread. It's sure to be a winner! Serve warm with mango butter as a treat with your morning coffee.

Servings: 2 loaves

2 cups sifted all-purpose flour

½ cup whole wheat flour

2 tsp. baking powder

½ tsp. baking soda

2 tsp. ground cinnamon

½ tsp. salt

½ cup butter or margarine

1 ¾ cups sugar

3 eggs

1 cup mashed mango (2 very ripe mangoes)

1 cup mashed avocado (4 ripe avocadoes)

½ cup chopped nuts

2 tsp. vanilla extract

Preheat oven to 350° F (180° C).

Grease two loaf pans well.

Sift together both flours, baking powder, baking soda, salt, and cinnamon. Set aside.

Cream together the butter and sugar. Add the eggs one at a time and whisk until light and fluffy.

Mix the mango and avocado puree together. Fold the dry ingredients into the fruit puree. Mix in the nuts and vanilla extract.

Pour the batter into the prepared loaf pans and bake for 1 hour, or until a knife inserted into the center of the bread comes out clean.

Cool the loaves for 10 to 15 minutes in the pan before removing and cooling completely on a wire rack.

Gingered Pumpkin Muffins

Did you know that Caribbean pumpkins are called Calabaza or Cuban squash? They are a bit different from the American pumpkins found during thanksgiving. Caribbean pumpkins or Calabaza are normally very large and varies in color to their orange counterparts being a green and white speckled color. They are sold in halves or quarters at most Hispanic and Caribbean Markets.

Servings: 12 muffins

1 cup butter

1 cup sugar

4 large eggs

1 tsp. vanilla extract

2 cups milk

½ cup sour cream

1 ½ cups sifted flour

2 tbsp. baking powder

2 tbsp. ground ginger

1 tsp. cinnamon powder

1 lb. pumpkin, peeled, cooked and mashed (you can substitute with 16oz. can pure pumpkin puree)

Preheat oven to 350° F (180° C).

Grease muffin tins and lightly dust with flour.

Cream butter and sugar together and add the eggs one at a time. Add the vanilla, milk and sour cream.

Mix together the flour, baking powder, ginger, and cinnamon and fold into the egg mixture along with the pumpkin. Mix lightly together to combine ingredients.

Drop batter into prepared muffin tins until about ¾ full. Lightly tap tin so that mixture settles evenly in pan.

Bake for 30 minutes or until the muffins move from the side of the pan and tops are brown.

Banana Coconut Muffins

One cannot visit the Caribbean and not find good banana muffins, With the early cultivating of bananas as one of its main exports, the Caribbean is blessed with an abundance of Bananas, even if bananas are no longer planted for exporting, Most of the local farmers still harvest it for the local markets.

Servings: 12 muffins

2 cups all-purpose flour

2/½ tsp. baking powder

½ tsp. salt

1 cup very ripe bananas, mashed (about 3 bananas)

½ cup milk

½ cup butter, melted

½ cup sugar

½ cup light brown sugar

2 eggs

1 cup coconut flakes

2 tsp. vanilla

1 tsp. cinnamon

½ tsp. grated nutmeg

Preheat oven to 350° F (180° C).

Lightly grease 12 muffin tins and flour lightly.

Sift together the flour, baking powder and salt. Set aside.

Combine the bananas with the milk.

In a separate bowl mix the melted butter with the sugars, add to the milk mixture, add the eggs one at a time and beat lightly.

Add the flour mixture to the banana mixture and fold in the coconut flakes, vanilla and spices. Stir lightly until all ingredients are combined.

Spoon into muffin cups and bake for 30 minutes, or until a toothpick inserted in the middle comes out clean.

"The Childhood Art of Picking Mango"

Growing up on the island of Dominica, mango season is in the early summer, as kids on our way home from school. We would gang up under the mango trees which were in every yard all over the village. (Sometimes with a dog tied to the tree to keep us away).

We would heap up stones for stoning the mangoes. The girls did the heaping, and the boys did the stoning. It was a game to see who would stone down the most mangoes. With stones flying everywhere there was always some busted heads. I had my share, but that could not put a damper on the joy of eating the mangoes. With the mango juice running all over your hands and clothes no one cared if they ended up with a beating when we got home late with mango stained uniforms. There are times when we make a mango bubbi (breast) by pounding the mango on a stone, rock or softening with a hand until the mango is soft. We then made a small hole in the top of the mango and sucked the juice out from the mango. That for me is still the best way to eat a mango, no napkin needed.

Spiced Sweet Plantain Bread

Plantain, which is part of the banana family, is used extensively in Caribbean cooking. It is used in the ripe or green stage. Plantains are used as a starch dish where it is cooked green, sliced or mashed. Most island cooks, however, cook it ripe where it is sliced and fried and served as a side dish. In this bread recipe the plantains are used in its very ripe stage (almost black), sliced, fried and then mashed. The result is a hearty-tasting Caribbean bread perfect with your morning coffee or as an afternoon snack.

Chef Freda

2 Large ripe plantains

1 tbsp. butter or margarine mixed with 1 tbsp. cooking oil

3 cups flour

1 ½ tsp. baking powder

1 tsp. baking soda

½ tsp. salt

1 tsp. cinnamon powder

½ tsp. grated nutmeg

½ tsp. ground all- spice

1 cup butter

1 cup sugar

1 egg

2 tsp. orange juice

1 tsp. orange or rum extract

Preheat the oven to 350° F (180° C).

Grease and lightly dust two loaf pans with flour, shaking off excess.

Peel and slice the plantains into medium-thin slices. Melt the butter with the vegetable oil over medium heat. Add the plantains and fry lightly on both sides until soft (without browning). Remove plantains and drain on kitchen towels to remove excess oil. Place in a small bowl and mash with a fork to form a soft paste.

In a large bowl add the flour, baking powder, baking soda, salt and spices.

Place the butter and sugar in a large mixing bowl and cream together until fluffy. Beat the eggs one at a time into the sugar mixture. Add the plantains, orange juice and orange extract and blend the mixture lightly.

Pour the batter into the prepared pans and bake in the oven for about a 45 minutes or until a knife inserted in the middle of the bread comes out clean.

Remove bread from the pan and cool before serving.

Cassava Pone

Cassava or Yucca as it is sometimes called on some of the islands is a starchy, root vegetable; it is covered in a dark bark like skin which has to be removed before using.

2 cups sweet cassava, peeled, washed & grated (about 2 large cassava)

2 cups grated coconut

2 tbsp. butter melted

¾ cup sugar

½ tsp. ground cinnamon

¼ tsp. salt

1 tsp. vanilla extract

3 cups water

Preheat oven to 350° F (180° C).

Grease a shallow casserole dish. Set aside.

Mix cassava with coconut, add butter, sugar, cinnamon, salt and vanilla extract. Combine together and add enough water to bind the mixture together. Pour mixture into prepared casserole dish.

Bake for 1 hour. The top should be brown and crisp.

Serve cut into squares.

Jamaican Cassava Bread Bammy Recipe

1 large sweet cassava (to make 2 cups)

pinch of salt

1 ½ cups coconut milk

Peel and grate the cassava. Place the grated cassava in a clean tea towel and wring out as much of the juice as you can. Add salt and mix together until combined. Divide the mixture up into one cup-sized portions. Flatten each portion out into a thick disc shape.

Heat a lightly oiled thick- bottomed skillet. Add the bammies to the skillet and fry each side over a medium heat for 9 minutes. Remove from the skillet and soak in coconut milk for 5 minutes. Place the bammies back in the pan and fry on both sides until they are a light brown color.

TOASTING METHOD

The bammy can also be cooked using the toasting method: this is done by broiling both sides of the bammy until brown. These are then served hot with butter or prepared salt fish.

ISLAND VARIATION

Bammies are called Bambula in Antigua are prepared similarly. The cakes are toasted and then split in two. Place the spiced sweet coconut between the two slices and serves hot.

Did you know that due to the early English, French and Spanish colonialists in the Caribbean islands lots of the local island recipes feature the cooking methods of these early colonial settlers flavored with locally grown ingredients?

Mango Pineapple Cinnamon Scones

3 cups all-purpose flour

⅓ cup granulated sugar

¾ tsp. salt

1 tbsp. baking powder

1 tsp. ground cinnamon

½ tsp. ground nutmeg

½ cup cold butter

2 large eggs

1 tsp. vanilla extract

½ cup crushed pineapple, drained

½ cup fresh pineapple, peeled and chopped

½ cup firm ripe mango, peeled and chopped

TOPPING

½ tsp. ground cinnamon

3 tbsp. coarse brown sugar

In A large bowl add the flour, sugar, salt, baking powder, cinnamon and nutmeg. Add the cold butter, cut into medium pieces, and work it into the flour mixture just until everything is unevenly crumbly: it's OK for some larger chunks of butter to remain unincorporated.

In a separate bowl whisk together the eggs, vanilla extract and crushed pineapples. Add these liquid ingredients to the dry ingredients. Add the chopped pineapple and mango and mix until all is moistened and holds together.

Line a baking sheet with parchment paper. If you don't have parchment just use it without greasing. Sprinkle a bit of flour on top of the parchment or pan.

Scrape the dough onto the floured parchment, or pan, and divide in half. Gently pat each half into a round disc.

Stir together the cinnamon and brown sugar.

Brush each circle with milk and sprinkle with the sugar topping.

Using a knife or pallet knife, that you've run under cold water, slice each circle into 6 wedges.

Carefully pull the wedges away from the center to separate them just a bit; there should be about ½□ space between them, at their outer edges.

Note: For the best texture and flakiness place the pan of scones in the freezer for 30 minutes, uncovered. This relaxes the gluten in the flour which makes the scones tenderer and allows them to rise higher. It also chills the fat which will make the scones a bit crumblier and flakier.

While the scones are chilling, preheat the oven to 425° F (220° C).

Bake the scones for 18 to 22 minutes, or until they're golden brown. When you pull one away from the others it should look baked all the way through; the edge shouldn't look wet or unbaked.

Remove the scones from the oven and cool briefly on the pan before transferring to a rack.

Dominica "Cush Cush" Yam Drop Biscuits

Yams are a staple in Caribbean cooking. They are usually medium to large roots which are edible. They are used mainly in soups and stews and can be served mashed or fried. In this unique recipe the yams used are cush-cush which has a softer and finer texture.

Servings: about 12 biscuits

¾ cup cooked cush-cush yams

½ tsp. salt

⅔ cup milk

3 tbsp. melted butter

1 ¼ cups flour

¼ tsp. baking powder

1 tsp. ground cinnamon

2 tbsp. brown sugar

Mash cush-cush yams while hot. Add milk and butter and mash together to combine and remove lumps. Allow mixture to cool.

Mix the flour, baking powder, cinnamon and sugar together. Add the flour mixture to the cush-cush and mix together to form a smooth paste, being careful not to over mix. Drop mixture from a tablespoon onto a greased baking tray.

Pre-heat the oven to 375° F (190° C). Bake the biscuits for 15 minutes, or until done.

Remove from the oven, cool slightly and serve warm.

Optionally serve sprinkled the tops with powdered sugar mixed with cocoa.

Papaya Passion Fruit Bread

1 cup firm ripe papaya, skin removed and chopped

1 cup fresh passion fruit juice (about 8 passion fruit)

1 ¼ cups sugar

½ cup vegetable oil

3 eggs

¼ cup milk

1 tsp. baking powder

½ tsp. baking soda

½ tsp. salt

3 cups flour

Preheat oven to 350° F (180° C).

Grease 2 loaf pans with butter or shortening and dust lightly with flour. Set aside.

Place the papaya in a small mixing bowl. In a large mixing bowl place the passion fruit juice, sugar, oil, eggs and milk mixture and stir until combined. Add the baking powder, soda, salt and flour and lightly fold in the papaya fruit. Pour batter into prepared loaf pan.

Bake the bread for 45 minutes to 1 hour, or until done. Test for doneness by inserting a knife in the center and if it comes out clean the bread is done.

Remove the bread from the pan and cool slightly before slicing.

Jonny Cakes

One of the quick and all-time island favorites is this quick and easy bread. Jonnycakes are served with early morning cocoa, tea, coffee or bush tea. Jonnycakes are also served with traditional Sunday morning breakfasts on some of the islands.

2 cups all-purpose flour

2 tsp. baking powder

1 tbsp. sugar

½ tsp. salt

1 tbsp. vegetable shortening

1 tbsp. butter

⅓ cup milk or water

canola oil for frying

Mix the flour, baking powder, sugar and salt in a bowl. Add the shortening and butter and blend the mixture with the fingertips until crumbly. Make a well in the center, add the milk and mix into a smooth, stiff dough. Do not over mix.

Place dough in a bowl and cover. Let dough sit for 15 minutes to relax the gluten.

Heat the oil in a large, heavy skillet to 400° F (200° C).

Cut dough into small pieces and form into balls by lightly rolling in the palm of the hands. Using fingers flatten balls lightly by pressing to form a disc and rest for 5 minutes.

Fry until golden brown on both sides; reduce heat as necessary.

Drain on paper towels and serve warm.

VARIATIONS

Jonnycakes Roasted: they can be roasted in a large stone pot on open coals and are called roast dumplings. More care must be taken when roasting since the heat and dumplings must be adjusted ensure that the insides are cooked.

Jonny Cakes Baked: on some islands, e.g. Trinidad, Jonnycakes are baked instead of fried. The water is substituted with coconut milk. After forming the dough it is then baked at 350° F (180° C) in a pre-heated oven for 20 minutes. It is served hot: sliced and buttered.

Do you know? That Roti was brought to the region by the East Indian contract laborers, as early as 1840, and has been localized as a Caribbean dish. Variations on roti are popular throughout the Caribbean and parts of South America.

Roti

Roti and Dahl Puri are Indian flatbreads found mostly on the islands of Trinidad and Guyana, which have a strong Indian influence on the island's local cuisine.

½ cups all-purpose flour

2 tsp. baking powder

¼ tsp. salt

1 tbsp. butter

1 cup water or milk

1 cup oil

Sift the flour, baking powder and salt together in a bowl. Add butter and incorporate lightly into the mixture with fingers. Add water, a little at a time, and knead into a soft dough, being careful not to over mix. The dough should not be sticky.

Cut dough into six pieces and form into balls. Rest the dough balls, covered, for 5 minutes to relax the dough.

On a floured surface, roll each ball into 8-inch circles. Brush each circle with a light coating of oil and sprinkle lightly with flour. Fold in half, then into a quarter, and then roll quarters into a ball. Cover dough and rest for 10 minutes.

Meanwhile, heat a heavy cast iron griddle until very hot.

Roll each ball in thin rounds and place on the hot griddle. Brush top and sides with oil to prevent sticking. Adjust heat so as not to burn. Turn the dough over frequently for even cooking.

Remove roti from griddle and with a clean towel pound between palms of your hands until pliable.

Serve roti warm with curries or other sauces.

Dali Puri

1 cup yellow split peas

2 cups water

1 tsp. salt

1 tsp. cayenne powder

2 garlic cloves, chopped

1 small onion, chopped

2 sprigs thyme

1 tsp. ground cumin

1 cup milk

2 cups flour

1 tsp. baking powder

1 tbsp. butter

Oil for brushing

Sort and wash split peas. Bring to the water to the boil in a large pot with added salt, pepper, cloves, onions and thyme. Cover pot and cook over medium heat until peas are tender and water has been absorbed. Remove thyme and grind peas in a food mill or blender while still hot. Add cumin and mix together. Set aside to cool.

Meanwhile, sift the flour with the baking powder and add the butter and enough milk to form soft and smooth dough.

Pre-heat a heavy iron griddle over medium heat.

Cut dough into golf-sized balls and roll out into round, medium-thick circles. Place a small spoonful of pea mixture into the center of the circles, flatten mixture slightly and then enclose into the dough.

Roll dough out thinly and cook on a heated griddle, brushing with oil to prevent sticking. Cook on both sides until golden brown.

Roti Variation

Paratha Roti: Roti made with butter, usually ghee, and also cooked on a tava. It can also be cooked on a large, flat cast iron skillet. Oil is rubbed on both sides and then it is fried, giving it a crisp outside. When it almost finished cooking, the roti is mashed while it is on the tava, causing it to crumble. I have also done it by placing in a clean towel and crumbling by hitting with a knife. It is also called 'Buss-Up-Shut' in Trinidad because it resembles a 'burst up shirt.'

Caribbean Corn and Coconut Bread

2 cups flour

½ cup sugar

1 ½ tbsp. baking powder

½ tsp. salt

1 tsp. ground cinnamon

½ tsp. ground nutmeg

1 cup medium grain yellow cornmeal

1 cup freshly grated coconut

½ cup butter, melted

1 cup milk

3 eggs, lightly beaten

Combine flour, sugar, baking powder, salt, cinnamon and nutmeg. Add and mix in the cornmeal and coconut. Combine the butter, milk and eggs and in a small bowl. Lightly fold into the flour mixture until thoroughly combined.

Pre-heat the oven to 350° F (180° C).

Place batter into the prepared pan and bake for 35 minutes until the bread leaves the sides of the pan when touched.

Serve warm with butter.

VARIATION

As a teen on the island of Antigua one of our elderly neighbors used to make a cake she called Cha Cha Dumplings. This was a corn and coconut mixture like this recipe. This she placed into greased pieces of banana leaves. The parcels were then tied to secure the mixture inside and baked on a large flat clay pot on open coals.

Why I wrote This Book

One of the reasons why I wrote this book as I traveled around the Caribbean islands, is that I am saddened to see a lot of the old recipes that were made by my parents, grandparents and great-grandparents slowly being lost with no way of preserving them for the future generations. I am always delighted when I see a local baker still producing those authentic island baking goods. With the development of tourism, lots of other ingredients are being added to these recipes to suit the international palate. Although I am grateful for tourism, I also want to see our Caribbean baking traditions preserved for the generations to come.

Chef Freda

Coconut Drops

This was one of my dad's favorites because it was sometimes made from let over flour, grated coconuts and whatever was left from the morning's baking went into this quick and easy cake. He loved it when it was left to bake a little longer and it became crispier around the edges.

Chef Freda

1 cup flour

½ cup sugar

1 tsp. baking powder

½ cup grated coconut

¼ cup raisin

¼ cup milk

¼ butter or margarine

¼ cup candied cherries

½ tsp. cinnamon

½ tsp. allspice

1 tsp. vanilla extract

1tsp. grated orange rind

2 tbsp. brown sugar for sprinkling on the top

Preheat oven to 400° F (200° C).

Grease a large cookie sheet and dust lightly with flour.

Combine in a large mixing bowl the flour and baking powder. Add the coconut, raisins, milk and butter and lightly mix together. Fold in the cherries, spices, vanilla extract and orange rind. Mix lightly to form stiff biscuit-like dough.

Drop a large spoonful onto the prepared cookie sheet and form into balls, leaving enough space in between so they do not touch each other. Sprinkle with brown sugar crystals and bake for 45 minutes, or until golden.

Remove from pan and cool before serving with jam and butter.

VARIATION

Rock Cakes: Rock cakes are made using the basic ingredients for coconut drops with the exclusion of the coconut. An extra ¼ cup of flour can be added to make a thicker dough and denser cake.

Sweet Potato Orange Muffins

1 cup butter

1 cup sugar

4 eggs

1 tsp. vanilla extract

2 cups orange juice

1 tsp. grated orange rind

1 cup sweetened condensed milk

2 cups flour, sifted

2 tbsp. baking powder

3 large sweet potatoes (1 lb.), peeled, cooked and mashed

Preheat the oven to 350° F (180° C).

Grease muffins tins and dust lightly with flour or spray with non-stick cooking spray.

Cream the butter and sugar together. Add the eggs one at a time, beating lightly after each one. Add the vanilla extract, orange juice, zest and milk. Fold in the flour, baking powder and the sweet potatoes.

Drop the batter into the prepared muffins tins are not more than ¾ full. Bake for 35 minutes, or until muffins are golden brown and move from the side of the tin when lightly pressed.

Cool a little and serve warm.

Sapodilla Nut Bread

1 stick butter, softened

1 cup brown sugar

½ cup vegetable oil

4 eggs, beaten

3 ¼ cups flour

2 tsp. baking soda

1 tsp. baking powder

2 tsp. ground cinnamon

2 tsp. ground allspice

1 tsp. ground nutmeg

1 cup sapodillas mashed

¼ cup sour cream (optional)

1 cup chopped walnuts

1 cup raisins

Cream the butter and sugar together. Mix in the oil. Add the eggs one at a time and beat well.

Sift together the flour, baking soda, cinnamon, allspice and nutmeg.

Mix the Sapodilla with the sour cream. Add the dry ingredients alternately with the sapodilla mixture.

Add the nuts and raisins and pour the mixture in a greased loaf pan.

Pre-heat the oven to 350° F (180° C). Bake the bread for one hour, or until a skewer inserted into the middle comes out clean.

Serve the bread warm and sliced.

Zucchini Bread

I love the ease of growing zucchini and my zucchini patch never fails to give me an abundant supply. This bread is easy and a joy to make

Chef Freda

Servings: 2 loaves

3 eggs, beaten

1 cup canola or vegetable oil

1 ½ cups sugar

2 cups zucchini, grated and well drained

2 tsp. vanilla extract

2 cups all-purpose flour

½ tsp. baking soda

1 ½ tsp. baking powder

½ tsp. salt

1 tbsp. ground cinnamon

1 tsp. ground nutmeg

1 cup chopped walnuts or other nuts

1 cup raisins

Preheat the oven to 350° F (180° C).

In a large bowl combine the beaten eggs, oil, sugar, zucchini and vanilla. Sift the flour, baking soda, baking powder, salt, cinnamon and nutmeg into the egg mixture. Stir in the walnuts and raisins and stir lightly to combine. Be careful not to over mix.

Pour the batter evenly into 2 lightly greased and floured loaf pans. Bake in the middle of the oven for 50-60 minutes.

Cool slightly before serving.

Barbados Coconut Bread

Wherever you travel in the Caribbean, you will always find a local coconut and banana bread served mostly as a tea, breakfast or lunch bread with each island adding its own spin to the basic ingredients. The following are two of my favorites.

Chef Freda

2 cups all-purpose flour

1 cup sugar

1 tbsp. baking powder

½ tsp. ground cinnamon

¼ tsp. ground cloves

¼ tsp. ground nutmeg 1 tsp. salt

1 ½ cups freshly grated coconut

1cup milk

2 tbsp. butter, melted

½ cup dried cherries (optional)

Preheat the oven to 350° F (180° C).

Grease 2 mini loaf pans or 1 large pan and dust lightly with flour or non-stick cooking spray.

In large bowl combine together the flour, sugar, baking powder, cinnamon, cloves and nutmeg. Add the grated nutmeg. Add the coconut and then the milk and butter. Lightly mix all ingredients together.

Pour into prepared pans and bake in the oven for 45 minutes to 1 hour, or until the bread begins to pull away from the sides of the pan.

Remove from pan and lightly cool.

Serve warm sliced with butter.

Jamaican Banana Bread

1 cup butter

1 cup sugar

2 eggs

3 very ripe medium bananas (1½ cups mashed banana)

2 cups all-purpose flour

1 tbsp. baking powder

1 tsp. ground cinnamon

¼ tsp. ground nutmeg

¼ tsp. salt

¼ cup milk

1 tsp. vanilla extract

¾ cup shelled pecan nuts or walnuts chopped

¼ cup golden raisins

Preheat the oven to 350° F (180° C).

Grease and lightly flour 2 loaf pans.

Cream together the butter and sugar. Add the eggs one at a time, lightly beating after each is added. Add the bananas.

Combine together the flour, baking powder, spices and salt. Add the flour mixture into the banana mixture along with the milk and vanilla extract.

Fold in the nuts and raisins and lightly mix to combine ingredients. Pour mixture into prepared pans.

Bake in pre-heated oven for 45 minutes, or until a knife inserted in the center comes out clean.

Cool bread lightly in the pan before removing and serving warm.

Coconut Facts and Tips

The Caribbean is known for its abundance of coconuts; the trees can be seen growing all across the islands. The milk of a coconut is the clear liquid you find when you open a green or dry coconut and makes a delicious, refreshing drink on a hot day. As the coconut ripens and the color changes from green to brown, the flesh starts becoming a jelly followed by the hard coconut flesh. Coconuts are used in Caribbean baking: grated for coconut milk, sugar candies, local desserts and drinks.

Orange Coffee Cake Doughnuts

Servings: 12 - 15 doughnuts

1 cup sugar

½ stick (4 tbsp.) butter

2 eggs

4 cups sifted all-purpose flour

1 tbsp. baking powder

1 tbsp. ground cinnamon

1 tsp. salt

3 tbsp. instant coffee powder

2 tbsp. hot water

1 tbsp. grated orange zest

¼ cup milk

vegetable oil for frying

cinnamon sugar for coating (3 tbsp. sugar mixed with 1 tbsp. ground cinnamon)

Cream the butter and the sugar together in a mixing bowl.

Add the eggs one at a time, beating well after each addition.

Sift the flour, baking powder, cinnamon and salt together.

Dissolve the coffee in hot water.

Add the flour to the egg mixture alternating with the coffee and milk.

Stir in the orange zest. Beat the dough well. It should be smooth and not sticky.

Cover the dough and refrigerate for 2-3 hours. The dough can also be made and refrigerated overnight.

Lightly flour a flat surface. Divide the dough in 2. Roll dough out on the floured surface. Cut the dough out with a doughnut cutter. Place cut dough on a lightly floured platter. If you don't have a doughnut cutter this can also be done by using a wide rim glass to cut out the circle and a small round cookie cutter to cut out the hole in the middle.

Gather the scraps, form into rounds and roll out. Continue until all dough is used up.

Heat the vegetable oil in a thick-bottomed pan or a deep-fat fryer to 375° F (190° C). Fry the doughnuts 4 - 6 at a time, being careful not to overcrowd the pot.

Fry the doughnuts until golden on one side and then turn over with tongs. Fry the other side until golden. Remove from the oil and drain on paper towels.

Roll the doughnuts in a bowl of cinnamon sugar.

Coconut Kisses

Servings: 20 -25

2 cups grated coconut

2 tbsp. sugar

⅓ cup condensed milk

zest of 1 lime, grated

Mix all ingredients together. Form the mixture into small cone shapes on a greased cookie sheet.

Bake the kisses in a preheated oven at 350° F (180° C) for 20 minutes, or until they are slightly brown.

Grandma B's Breakfast Grits

I include this recipe for grits in memory of my mother-in-law, grandma B, who loved to prepare grits whenever she visited. Even though it was not a staple at our house, my kids always enjoyed it whenever she prepared it

Chef Freda

1½ cups water

½ cup heavy cream

½ cup half n half (you can use milk but the grits will be less creamy)

½ cup 5-minute grits

2 tbsp. butter

salt and pepper

Add water, heavy cream, half and a half to a pot. Bring to a boil.

Slowly add the grits whilst whisking steadily. Reduce heat to low and cover.

Cook for 5 - 7 minutes, whisking frequently and remove from heat.

Add butter and salt and pepper to taste.

Serve while still hot. The grits go great with fried eggs, bacon or corned beef.

Caribbean Christmas Ginger Bread Loaf

Servings: 10

½ cup molasses

1 cup sugar

½ cup butter

½ cup pineapple juice

½ cup mixed fruit (raisin & mixed peel that has been soaked in rum)

2 ⅓ cups flour

1 ½ tsp. baking powder

½ tsp. baking Soda

1 tsp. ground cinnamon

1 tsp. ground nutmeg

2 tbsp. freshly grated ginger

1 egg, lightly beaten

Preheat the oven to 350° F (180° C).

Grease and lightly dust with flour a medium loaf pan or 2 small loaf pans.

Heat the molasses, sugar, butter and pineapple juice over medium heat. Add the fruit mixture and set aside to cool.

In a mixing bowl sift together the flour, baking powder, baking soda, cinnamon and nutmeg. Stir in the ginger and egg.

Mix the cool molasses mixture into the flour mixture and lightly fold in ingredients until combined.

Pour into the prepared pan and bake for about 45 minutes, or until a knife or skewer comes out clean when inserted in the middle of the loaf.

Cool lightly in pan.

Serve sliced with butter.

Virgin Islands Baked Coconut Dumb Bread

My husband, Freeston, lived in the Virgin Islands for a while and whenever I visited it was always a treat to buy this delicious sweet bread at the local island bakery. It is really quick and easy to make with no special trimmings. This is a great breakfast bread.

Chef Freda

Servings: 8-10

2 cups all-purpose flour

2 tsp. baking powder

¼ tsp. baking soda

1 tsp. ground cinnamon

1 tsp. ground Nutmeg

3 tbsp. sugar

¼ cup vegetable shortening

2 tbsp. salted butter

1 ½ cups grated fresh coconut

¼ cup coconut milk

½ cup evaporated milk

Preheat the oven to 350° F (180° C).

Lightly grease a cookie sheet and set aside.

Add to a medium bowl the flour, baking powder, baking soda and sugar. Cut in the shortening and butter until mixture is crumbly. Add the cinnamon and nutmeg.

Add coconut and mix in until incorporated.

Mix both milks together and add to the flour mixture slowly until stiff dough is formed. Knead the dough for 5 -10 minutes until the dough is smooth.

Dust the dough lightly with flour, cover with a towel and leave to rest for 15 minutes.

Cut the dough in two and knead lightly on a floured surface. Form the dough into two logs and press lightly with hands to flatten.

Place dough on a cookie sheet. Bake in the oven for 20 - 30 minutes, or until golden. The bread is done when a toothpick inserted in the center comes out clean.

Serve warm with butter.

Jamaican Bulla

2 ¾ cups brown sugar

½ tbsp. salt

2 cups plus 2 tbsp. water

1 cup margarine

2 tbsp. ginger

2 tbsp. vanilla

7 ½ cups flour

3 tbsp. baking powder

½ tbsp. baking soda

1 tsp. nutmeg

flour for rolling the bulla

Pre-heat the oven to 375° F (190° C).

Dissolve sugar and salt in water. Add ginger, margarine and vanilla.

Sift together all dry ingredients and gradually combine with the liquid.

Dough must be sticky and heavy. Place dough on a floured board and dust with flour until dough is manageable and does not stick to fingers.

Roll out to a thickness of about ⅓" and cut into slices.

Bake bulla for 20 - 25 minutes, or until cooked through and golden brown.

Yeast Breads

So the people took their dough before it was leavened, having their kneading bowls bound up in their clothes on their shoulders.

Exodus 12: 34

Story: "The Pig, the Bun, Sharon and Me"

My friend Sharon and I were famous for secretly talking and giggling; we were always up to something. One night, when everyone was inside our house, we sneaked out and headed up to the local grocery store. We were on our way to buy bun, butter and cheese (one of the most popular village night time snacks) and we decided that we were not going to share with anyone. After pooling our meager savings together we purchased a large order of bun, butter and cheese and headed back home. On our return home we hid our purchased snack in one of our garden flower pots and we went inside to see if everyone was asleep or otherwise occupied. After the way was clear and we could eat without any chance of sharing, or other disturbances, we headed back to retrieve our prized snack. To our dismay we couldn't find our hidden snack. After a frenzied look, we heard some paper crumbling and a scuffling sound. Low and behold our pig had just found himself dinner and had eaten our hidden snack!

Chef Freda

Antigua Sunday Bread

Antiguans bakers pride themselves with their breads especially the Sunday bread made by the local Antigua Bakeries. Sunday breads are the cream of the crop; extra richness is added with the addition of vegetable shortening or lard which produces more delicate and richer-tasting breads. The breads are also formed into larger loaves with decorative plaits and twists on top of the crust. These Sunday breads are great accompaniments to the traditional Antigua Sunday breakfast of stewed salt fish and chopped eggplant.

Chef Freda

2 tbsp. quick rising yeast (or 2 ¼ oz. packages)

3 tbsp. sugar

3 cups lukewarm water

6 cups all-purpose flour plus 1 cup for dusting and kneading

¾ cup vegetable shortening

2 tbsp. lard or butter

2 tsp. salt

Preheat the oven to 350° F (180° C).

Grease 2 large cookie sheets and set aside.

In a medium bowl, add the yeast, sugar and water. Cover and let sit for 10 - 15 minutes until the mixture is bubbly.

In a large bowl sift the flour and form a well in the center. Add the shortening, lard, and salt. Pour in the yeast and mix into a smooth dough. The dough should not be sticky.

Cover and let rise until dough doubles its size, about 45 minutes to 1 hour. Place dough on a floured surface and knead for 5 minutes. Dust lightly with flour, cover and let rise for another 45 minutes to 1 hour, or until dough doubles in size.

Cut dough into 4 large pieces and roll into balls. Rest for another 15 minutes to relax the dough. Cut a small piece from each circle to decorate the top of the loaves.

Form dough into 4 large long loaves. Beginning from the middle, fold dough in a half circle and roll on a lightly floured surface with palm of the hands until a nice loaf is formed. Place on a greased cookie sheet, being careful that the seam is at the bottom of the pan.

Using the small piece that was left from each loaf, roll each piece into a long strip, cut strips into 3 pieces, join together at one end and plait into a long braid.

Brush top of bread lightly with water and place braid on top of each loaf. Secure each end by pressing securely into top of the loaves. Cover loaves and let rise for 10 -15 minutes, or until loaves are double in size.

Bake until golden, or the loaf sounds hollow when tapped on the bottom.

Whole Wheat Herbed Yeast Biscuits

Servings: 24 biscuits

1 packet dry yeast

⅓ cup warm water

2 ½ cups whole wheat flour

½ cup all-purpose flour plus 2 tbsp. for dusting

½ tsp. baking powder

½ tsp. baking soda

½ tsp. salt

1 tbsp. sugar

½ tsp. chopped thyme

½ tsp. chopped basil

½ tsp. chopped oregano

3 tbsp. margarine

¾ cup milk

¼ cup plain yogurt

In a small bowl dissolve the yeast in the warm water. Let stand for 5 minutes.

In a large bowl or a stand-up mixer add the wheat flour, all-purpose flour, baking powder, baking soda, salt, sugar, thyme, basil and oregano.

Add the margarine and mix into the flour mixture until it resembles coarse meal.

Add the yeast mixture, milk and yogurt to the flour mixture and stir lightly together until ingredients are combined. Be careful not to over mix.

Sprinkle some of the remaining flour on the top of a flat surface and lightly knead the dough.

Roll the dough out to 2" thickness and cut into circles using a round cookie cutter or the rim of a wide mouth bottle or glass.

Place rounds on a lightly greased cookie sheet.

Bake in a preheated oven at 375° F (190° C) for 10 - 15 minutes, or until golden.

Remove from sheet cool lightly and serve warm.

Yeast Doughnuts with Pina Colada Glaze

Servings: 30 - 40 doughnuts

DOUGHNUTS

1 ¾ cups warm water plus 1 cup water

2 packets of active dry yeast

3 ¾ cups sifted all -purpose flour plus extra for dusting

¾ tsp. salt

vegetable oil for frying

2 cups coconut flakes to sprinkle on the top

GLAZE

2 cups confectioners' sugar

2 tbsp. rum

2 tbsp. Coco Lopez (coconut syrup)

2 tbsp. pineapple juice

In a large bowl combine the 1 ¾ cups water with the yeast and let stand for 5 minutes, or until bubbly.

Gradually mix in the 3 ¾ cup flour, 2 tbsp. sugar and the salt. Mix into a smooth dough.

Turn the dough out onto a floured surface and knead lightly until the dough is silky.

Lightly oil a medium bowl and add the dough. Cover and let rise in a warm place until dough has doubled its size, about 1 ½ hours.

Punch dough down and cover and let it rise again for another 20 - 30 minutes.

Make the Glaze whilst the dough is rising. In a bowl, whisk all the glaze ingredients together, cover and set aside.

In a large, thick bottomed pan, or sauce pan or a deep fryer, heat the oil to 350° F (180° C).

Cut the dough into quarters and roll each quarter out flat on a floured surface. Using a doughnut cutter cut dough into doughnut shapes (you can also use a wide rimed glass and a small round cutter for the middle).

Carefully add the doughnuts into the hot fat and fry on both sides until golden, about 1 minute on each side. Do not to overcrowd the pot.

Remove the doughnut with tongs and drain on paper towels.

Dip one side of the doughnut into the glaze and sprinkle with coconut flakes.

Pineapple Bread

This is a unique way to use fresh pineapples. The bread can be served as a breakfast or brunch bread and will make a great addition to your picnic baskets.

Servings: 12

1 packet (¼ oz.) dry yeast

½ cup lukewarm milk

½ cup sugar

2 ¼ cups all-purpose flour

½ cup (1 stick) butter, at room temperature

pinch of salt

1 cup raisins

1 small pineapple (about 1 lb.) peeled, cored and thinly sliced

1 cup of pineapple jam

1 tbsp. water

In a medium bowl add the yeast to the lukewarm milk and leave to stand until bubbly, about 10 minutes.

Sift the flour into a large bowl. Add the yeast mixture and mix together to form smooth dough.

Cover and leave in a warm place to rise until double, about 30 minutes.

Lightly beat the butter with a hand whisk.

Punch the dough down and then work in the butter, sugar and salt into the dough. Knead well until fully combined.

Lightly flour a rolling pin and use to roll out dough.

Lightly grease a 10" round cake pan and use the rolled out dough to line the pan, being careful to press in the corners to secure. Leave dough to prove for 15 - 20 minutes.

Soak the raisins in a small saucepan with warm water to plump; drain well before use.

Spread the pineapple slices evenly over the top of the dough and then sprinkle the raisins on the top.

Bake the bread in a preheated oven at 350° F (180° C) for 45 minutes, or until golden.

Remove from the oven. Mix the pineapple juice with the water and bring to a simmer stir until mixture is combined.

Spread the jam over the top carefully, making sure to cover the fruit well. Serve warm as a breakfast or brunch bread.

Jamaican Hard Dough Bread

4 tbsp. yeast (2 ¼ oz. packets)

4 cups lukewarm water

6 cups all-purpose flour

½ cup dry powdered milk or 1 cup evaporated milk

4 tbsp. sugar

2 tbsp. vegetable shortening or butter

sugar wash for the top (2 tbsp. sugar dissolved in 1 cup water)

Preheat oven to 350° F (180° C).

Prepare 2 loaf pans by lightly greasing.

In a large bowl dissolve the yeast in the water. Let mixture sit until yeast is bubbly.

In another bowl add flour, milk, sugar, salt and butter and with fingertips combine butter into flour mixture.

Make a well in the center and pour in the yeast mixture. Incorporate all the ingredients together. Pour mixture onto a floured surface and knead to stiff dough. Return the dough to a large bowl and cover with a towel. Let dough rise in a warm place for 1 - 1 ½ hours, or until the dough doubles in size.

Punch dough down to get the excess air out and cut into equal halves. Roll each half into a ball, cover and rest for 20 minutes. Form each half into loaves and place onto prepared loaf pans. Cover and let dough rise in a warm place for 1- 1 ½ hours until dough has doubled its size.

Bake in the oven for about 20 minutes.

Remove loaves from the pan and brush with the sugar mixture.

Cool before serving.

Curacao Jewish Challah Bread

Did you know?

The first Jewish settlers arrived in Curacao in 1651 from Amsterdam. They were followed by a larger Jewish group which arrived in 1659. The settled Jews were given the rights to practice their religion and were also provided extensive land grants, freedom from taxation and protection. Curacao boasted one of the oldest Jewish synagogue and Jewish cemeteries in the Caribbean region.

6 cups all-purpose flour (plus 2 cups for kneading)

2 tbsp. yeast

2 cups lukewarm water

1 cup golden raisins

2 large eggs, beaten

½ cup sugar

½ tsp. baking powder

½ tsp. ground cinnamon

1 tsp. vanilla extract

½ tbsp. salt

½ cup vegetable oil

GLAZE

1 egg

½ tbsp. sugar

Preheat oven to 350° F (180° C).

Grease a large cookie sheet or 2 large loaf pans and set aside.

Mix the yeast with 1 cup of flour and 1 cup of water until the yeast dissolves. Set mixture aside until mixture is bubbly, about 30 minutes.

Add the rest of the flour and water along with the other ingredients and knead mixture into dough. The dough will be sticky.

Add the extra flour, a little at a time, and knead until the dough is no longer sticky. Cover the dough, set aside and rest for 20 minutes. Lightly knead dough for 3 minutes, cover and rest for 25 minutes.

Cut dough into four large pieces and form into round loaves, or form dough into 2 large plaited braids. Place loaves on a cookie sheet or loaf pans and let rise until double in size.

Beat the egg with the sugar and brush the tops with the mixture.

Bake loaves for 45 minutes to 1 hour.

Serve warm with honey.

Bimini Honey Bread

I had pleasure of trying this bread while working for a short time at the Calypso Restaurant in Delray Beach Florida. It was one of my favorite items on the menu and also a great breakfast or lunch bread. I adjusted and recreated the recipe at home, and the result was nice light buttery bread filled with the gooey sweetness of the honey on the inside.

Chef Freda

2 packets of quick rising yeast (¼ oz. each)

2 cups water

6 cups all-purpose flour

¼ cup powdered milk

1 tsp. salt

2 tbsp. butter

2 eggs

2 tbsp. sugar

1 cup all natural organic honey

2 tbsp. melted butter.

Preheat oven to 350° F (180° C).

Grease 2 loaf pans and set aside.

In a medium bowl combine the yeast and water, cover and set aside until the mixture is bubbly.

In a large bowl sift the flour, powdered milk and salt. Mix in butter by hand.

In a small bowl beat the eggs and sugar until combined. Mix with the yeast mixture and combine into the flour mixture.

Knead on a floured surface into soft and smooth dough. Cover dough with a towel and let rest for 30 minutes, or until doubled in size. Divide dough into two equal pieces and form into balls. Cover and let stand for 20 minutes.

On a floured surface roll dough pieces into squares with a rolling pin. The length should be about ½" longer than the loaf pans. Cover one side with honey being careful not to get too close to the edges and oozes out.

Roll dough up in jelly roll style, close edges by pressing firmly with a finger and carefully place on loaf pans. Cover and set aside for 30 minutes to rise until doubled in size.

Brush tops with melted butter.

Bake for 45 minutes to 1 hour.

Leave loaves to cool for 10 minutes in the pan before removing.

Serve sliced and warm.

Cuban Bread

Cuban bread is perfect for making sandwiches due to its lightness. It is best served warm with spicy and rich flavor meats. Or as a pressed sandwich of Cuban Roast pork, sweet pickle, mustard the classic Cuban pressed sandwich.

2 packets dry yeast (½ oz. each)

4 tsp. sugar

2 cups lukewarm water

6 cups flour plus 1 cup for dusting

½ tbsp. salt

4 tbsp. olive oil or melted butter

1 egg lightly beaten with 1 tsp. of water for glazing tops

Grease 2 large loaf pans with butter or olive oil and set aside.

Dissolve the yeast in one cup of water in a bowl. Set aside for 5 minutes, or until the mixture is bubbly.

In a large mixing bowl place the flour and salt. Make a well in the center and add the olive oil and yeast mixture. Slowly add the rest of the water and mix into smooth, soft dough. Dough should not be sticky.

Place the dough on a lightly floured surface and knead the dough for 5 minutes. Place the dough in a large bowl, cover and place in a cool place and let the dough rise for 25 minutes. Punch dough down to remove excess air. Divide dough into loaves and place in loaf pans. Brush tops with egg mixture.

With a sharp knife make 3 cuts on top of loaves. Place loaves in cold oven and set the oven to 375° F (190° C). Bake for 45 minutes to 1 hour.

Remove bread from pan, check for doneness by tapping on the bottom of bread. If it sounds hollow the bread is done.

Cool the bread slightly. Serve hot.

Honey Grain Bread

Servings: 2 loaves

2 packets active dry yeast

½ cup warm water

⅓ cup honey

1 cup milk

¼ cup margarine

¼ cup frozen egg substitute, thawed (3 eggs whites)

½ cup bulgur wheat

½ cup wheat germ

1 tsp. salt

½ tsp. ground nutmeg

1½ cups whole wheat flour

4½ cups all -purpose flour

In a large bowl dissolve the yeast in the warm water, stir in 2 tbsp. honey and let stand for 5 minutes, or until bubbly.

In a small saucepan over medium heat combine the remaining honey, milk and margarine and stir until margarine is melted. Remove from heat to cool.

Add the milk mixture, egg substitute, bulgur, wheat germ, salt, nutmeg, whole wheat flour and 3 cups of the all-purpose flour.

Gradually mix ingredients to form stiff dough.

Sprinkle some reserved flour over the work surface and knead dough until smooth and elastic (about 8 - 10 minutes).

Place dough in a bowl, dust with flour and cover with a towel. Leave to rise in a warm place until doubled in size.

Punch dough down and divide in half. Roll dough on a floured surface and form into loafs. Tuck in edges. Repeat procedure with the other half of dough. Place loaves in two lightly greased loaf pans.

Cover and let rise in a warm place until doubled in size.

Pre-heat the oven to 350° F (180° C).

Bake loafs for 25 minutes, or until loafs sounds hollow when tapped on the bottom.

Remove loaves from pans and place on a wire rack to cool.

Because there is one loaf, we who are many are one body for we all partake of the one loaf.

Corinthians 10:17

Bahamas Anise Breakfast Bread

1 lb. flour

¼ lb. corn starch

1 – 2 tsp. anise or fennel seeds

2 packets yeast

1 tsp. baking powder

water

pinch of salt

Combine the flour and cornstarch with the water and add yeast, baking powder and a pinch of salt. Mix until a thick dough is formed.

Knead the dough until it gets smooth. Gather it into a ball. Add a little more flour, if necessary, so that it doesn't stick to your fingers.

Flatten the dough with your hand, sprinkle the anise or fennel seeds over the top and knead again.

Form into a ball once again and let rise 3 hours.

With a sharp knife, cut a crisscross pattern onto the surface of the bread to facilitate baking.

Place in a very hot oven to bake for 30 minutes.

Caribbean Butter Flap Bread

3 packets yeast

2 cups milk

5 cups flour

3 tbsp. sugar

4 oz. margarine

1 tsp. salt

2 eggs

4 oz. margarine or butter, melted (for basting)

Mix dry ingredients, yeast, sugar, flour, and salt in a large bowl.

Melt margarine and milk in microwave oven on low, or in a small saucepan. Add to dry ingredients. Stir well and then add eggs. Mix with mixer until smooth and the mixture leaves side of bowl. Cover bowl with a clean towel and place in a warm place and leave for 1 hour, or until mixture doubles in size.

Turn out on floured board or surface. Divide into 18 pieces and knead into balls. Cover and leave for 20 minutes.

Roll out very thinly and brush with melted margarine or butter. Fold in half and then in half again, into a triangular shape. Seal edges and prick with a fork. Place on greased cookie trays.

Bake in the oven at 325° F (165° C) for 25 minutes. Change shelves and increase heat to 375° F (190° C). Bake for another 20 minutes, or until golden.

Brush with melted margarine or butter while still hot.

Honor the Lord with your wealth and with the first fruits of all your crops, then your barns will be filled to overflowing, and your vats will brim over with new wine.

Proverbs 3: 9-10

Antiguan Coconut Raisins Buns

These are an all-time island favorite! They are great eaten on their own, however most Antiguans enjoy them served hot with butter and cheese.

Chef Freda

3 packets fast acting yeast (¼ oz. packets)

2 tbsp. sugar

2 cups lukewarm water

6 cups flour plus 1 cup for dusting

2 cups sugar

1 cup brown sugar

1 cup milk

¼ cup vegetable shortening

2 tbsp. butter

1 ½ cup freshly grated coconut

1 cup golden raisins

2 tsp. ground cinnamon

1 tsp. ground nutmeg

2 tsp. vanilla extract

2 tbsp. water for brushing top

2 tbsp. brown sugar for sprinkling on top

Preheat the oven to 350° F (180° C).

Grease a large cookie sheet with vegetable shortening or non-stick spray.

In a large bowl dissolve the yeast and sugar. Cover and let sit until mixture is bubbly.

Place the flour into a large bowl, make a well in the center and add the sugars, milk, shortening, butter, coconut, raisins, spices and vanilla extract. Pour in the yeast mixture and combine the mixture together. Dough will be slightly sticky. Dust with extra flour and form into a ball. Cover the dough and let sit until it doubles in size.

Punch dough back and knead for 2 minutes. Cover dough and let rest for 20 minutes. Cut dough into 6 large pieces and form into balls. Place on the cookie sheet and press lightly with palm of hands. Cover buns and let rise for 20 minutes until doubles in size. Score top of buns with a sharp knife by cutting 4 slits on top of buns.

Brush lightly with water and sprinkle with brown sugar.

Bake in oven for 35 - 45 minutes, or until golden and when tapped on the bottom it sounds hollow sound.

Remove from pan, cool lightly and serve warm.

Hot Cross Buns

Easter in the Caribbean is a time of celebration and it's one of the times I can remember as a kid that we always got the pleasure of wearing a new dress to church. Easter is also the time when traditional Easter dishes are served and one of these dishes is hot cross buns, made with the traditional icing cross on the top.

Chef Freda

3 cups all-purpose flour

3 tsp. baking powder

2 large eggs

1 cup sugar

½ cup brown sugar

1 cup milk

1 cup golden raisins

1 tsp. ground cinnamon

1 tsp. orange extract

2 tbsp. grated orange zest

2 tbsp. grated lime zest

ICING

1 cup icing sugar mixed with 2 tbsp. orange juice

Preheat the oven to 350° F (180° C).

Grease a large cookie sheet with vegetable shortening or non-stick cooking spray.

In a large bowl sift the flour and baking powder and make a well in the center. Add all the other ingredients and mix into a stiff batter.

Using a large spoon cut buns into medium pieces and place on cookie sheet, touching slightly.

Bake in the oven for 30 minutes, or until brown.

Remove from oven and cool slightly before glazing with icing glaze.

How to Open a Coconut for grated Coconut

Use a small hammer or large rock to open a coconut. First, with a clean nail or ice pick, puncture the two eyes at the top of the coconut. Drain the liquid into a small bowl. Using the hammer give the shell a hard blow to split it, or crack the shell by hitting it hard on a sturdy rock. This will cause the shell to fall away or break into pieces. Using a small, blunt knife cut the meat away from the shell. Wash the coconut meat thoroughly to remove the leftover shell. Before grating the coconut peel off the thin brown outer skin, cut the meat into smaller pieces and grate using a hand-held grater.

Jamaican Coco Bread

I first tasted coco bread when I lived in Ft Lauderdale Florida, My friend Neville used to buy them from his local Jamaican Bakery and got me hooked. The light, rich butter taste with the tropical flavor of coconut, Makes these great for sandwiches or as a dinner roll.

Chef Freda

2 packets dry yeast

¾ cup sugar

1½ cups lukewarm water

1 tsp. salt

½ cup butter

2 cups coconut milk

6 cups flour

¼ stick butter, softened

Preheat the oven to 350° F (180° C).

Grease or spray with non-stick cooking spray 2 large cookie sheets.

Dissolve the yeast and sugar in the lukewarm water. Cover and leave to rest until mixture is bubbly.

Heat the coconut milk with ½ cup of butter. Do not overheat.

Place the flour in a large bowl and make a well in the center. Add the yeast mixture and the coconut mixture. Lightly combine until a dough forms. Remove the dough from the bowl and place onto a floured surface and knead until smooth, about 10 minutes. Do not overmix.

Leave the dough sit covered for 10 - 15 minutes.

Cut dough into ½ in pieces and form into rolls. Roll each ball into circles about ⅓" thick. Brush the top of the circles with softened butter. Fold each circle in half and then into quarters.

Leave the rolls to rise for 30 minutes, or until doubled in size.

Bake for 20 – 25 minutes, or until cooked and golden.

Lightly brush the tops with butter while still hot.

"My Take on Faith"

Author Anonymous

My life is but a weaving
Between my God and me;
I do not choose the colors
He worketh steadily.
Oft' times He weaveth sorrow
And I, in foolish pride
Forget He sees the upper,
And I see the underside.
Not till the loom is silent
And the shuttles cease to fly,
Shall God unroll the canvas
And explain the reason why.
The dark threads are as needful
In the Weaver's skillful hand,
As the threads of gold and silver
In the pattern He has planned.

Mexican Sweet Bread Conchas

BREAD

½ tsp. yeast

½ cup warm water

½ cup evaporated milk

6 tbsp. white sugar

1 tsp. salt

⅓ cup butter or margarine, melted

1 egg

4 cups all-purpose flour

½ tsp. ground cinnamon

TOPPING

⅔ cup white sugar

½ cup butter or margarine

1 cup all-purpose flour

2 tsp. ground cinnamon

1 tsp. vanilla extract

Stir together the yeast and warm water in a large bowl. Mix in the milk, sugar, melted butter, salt, egg and half of the flour. Gradually mix in the remaining flour and cinnamon.

Turn the dough out onto a floured surface as soon as it pulls together enough. Knead for 6 to 8 minutes, or until smooth and elastic. Place in a large greased bowl and turn the dough to coat. Cover and let rise in a warm place until doubled in size, about 1 hour.

Make the topping while the dough rises. In a medium bowl beat sugar and butter until light and fluffy. Stir in the flour until the mixture is the consistency of thick paste. Divide into two parts and place in a separate bowls. Mix cinnamon into one-half and vanilla into the other half.

When the dough is done rising cut into 12 even-sized pieces. Shape into balls and place on a greased cookie sheet, spacing about 3 inches apart.

Divide each bowl of topping into 6 balls and pat flat. Place circles of topping on top of the dough balls, patting down lightly. Use a knife to cut grooves in the topping like a clam shell.

Cover and let rise until doubled, about 45 minutes.

Preheat the oven to 375° F (190° C).

Bake for 20 minutes, or until lightly golden brown.

Trinidad Hops Whole Wheat Bread

This recipe was adapted from the Naparima Girls Cookbook.

Servings: 12 – 14 hops

1 packet dry yeast

2 tsp. sugar

1 tbsp. melted shortening

4 cups white flour

2 cups whole wheat flour

2 ½ cups warm water

2 tsp. salt

Pour warm water into a large bowl.

Dissolve sugar in water.

Dissolve yeast in sugar and water and leave to develop for 10 minutes.

Stir yeast mixture with a fork and add melted shortening.

Gradually stir in flour and salt.

Knead for 8 to 10 minutes, adding flour if necessary to make medium stiff dough.

Grease a bowl and the top of the dough. Cover and leave to rest for 20 - 25 minutes.

Punch down dough and form into balls. Place on greased trays.

Bake in a 400° F (200° C) oven for 15 minutes.

For God is the one who provides food for the farmer and then bread to eat. In the same way he will provide and increase your resources and then produce a great harvest of generosity in you.

II Corinthians 9:10

Dominican Republic Pan de Coco (Coconut Bread)

Slightly sweet, coconut-enriched yeast bread from the island of Dominican Republic, Pan de Coco is perfect for breakfast or a snack, and can also be used as a dinner roll.

½ cup warm water (wrist-temperature)

3 tbsp. sugar

1 packet dry yeast (2¼ tsp.)

½ cup unsweetened shredded coconut

3 ½ cups all-purpose flour plus extra for kneading

½ tsp. fine salt

1 cup canned unsweetened coconut milk

3 tbsp. salted butter, softened, plus extra to grease the pan

Combine the warm water, sugar and yeast in a glass bowl. Stir to dissolve and cover to keep warm. Leave until bubbly, about 10 minutes.

Add the coconut and let it sit uncovered for 5 more minutes.

Combine the flour and salt in a large bowl. Pour the yeast mixture and coconut milk into the bowl with the flour. Stir together with a wooden spoon until the dough starts to come together.

Turn the dough out onto a floured board and knead the softened butter into the dough. After incorporating the butter continue to knead for 5 minutes on a wooden board. Add extra flour if necessary: the dough does not generally stick due to the fat content.

Form the dough into a ball and let it rest, covered with a damp kitchen cloth, in a warm place until doubled in size, about 1 ½ hours.

Split the dough into two balls and roll each into eight balls. Place each set of 8 balls in either a buttered 8" round cake pan (if you like them to stick together and be slightly softer) or on a buttered cookie sheet (if you prefer them to be separate and a bit crustier).

Pre-heat the oven to 350° F (180° C).

Let the rolls rise another 30 minutes, covered with a damp kitchen cloth, in a warm place.

Bake for 25 minutes.

Serve warm as a snack or with a meal instead of a dinner roll.

Dominica Mastiff Bread

Mastiff bread is one of the local breads served all over the island of Dominica. I can remember as a child my parents making it in their local bakery. It's a dense and sweeter loaf that is great serving on its own or as a sandwich. I have adjusted the recipe to make it a bit sweeter and lighter. However, this recipe can be adjusted if you are looking for a sweeter or heavier texture

Chef Freda

BREAD SPONGE

1½ cups lukewarm water

½ tsp. active dry yeast

1 tsp. sugar

3 ½ cups bread flour

FOR BREAD

2 cups plus 1 tbsp. lukewarm

1¼ tsp. active dry yeast

1 cup sponge, pulled into small pieces (recipe above)

7 cups bread flour

¼ cup sugar

¼ cup vegetable shortening

1 tbsp. salt

BREAD SPONGE (Makes about 3 ½ cups)

In electric mixer combine ¼ cup water, yeast and sugar. Let stand until yeast is creamy, about 10 minutes.

Add remaining water and flour, mixing on low speed for 2 minutes. It will be the consistency of wet dough.

Place in a lightly oiled bowl. Cover and let stand at room temperature for 24 hours. If refrigerated or frozen, bring to room temperature before using.

The sponge can be refrigerated for one week or frozen for up to three months.

THE BREAD

In electric mixer combine ¼ cup water and yeast. Let stand until yeast is creamy, about 10 minutes. Add ½ cup more water and sponge. Mix on low speed using paddle attachment for about 2 minutes.

Add flour, sugar, shortening, salt and remaining water. Mix for another 1 minute.

Use the dough hook and mix on medium-low speed, pulling dough from hook two or three times, until dough is soft and sticks to fingers when squeezed, about 8 minutes. Or knead by hand, 15 to 20 minutes.

On a floured work surface knead dough into a ball by hand, about four or five turns. Place smooth side up in a lightly oiled bowl. Cover with plastic wrap. Let rise in a warm place until tripled in size, about 1 ½ hours.

Turn dough onto floured surface. Flour top and cut in half. Roll up one piece of dough lengthwise, flatten slightly and roll lengthwise again. Using the palm of both hands form dough into long loafs.

On an un-floured surface, cup your hands around the sides of the dough and move it in small, circular motions until the top of dough is rounded and bottom is smooth.

Flour a piece of parchment and place dough on it, cover loosely with oiled plastic wrap and then cover with a towel. Repeat process with the second piece of dough.

Leave to rise in a warm place until doubled in size, about 50 minutes.

Thirty minutes before the final rise is completed place a baking stone or baking sheet in the oven and an empty baking pan on the lowest shelf. Heat the oven to °350 F (180° C).

Sprinkle dough with flour and dimple the surface with your fingertips and let rise for another 10 minutes.

Use a baker's peel or baking sheet to slide the loaves and parchment onto the baking stone or baking sheet. Pour 2 cups of very hot water into the heated baking pan to create steam.

Bake for 25 to 30 minutes, or until dark golden brown and hollow sounding when tapped on the bottom.

Transfer to a wire rack and cool for at least 30 minutes before slicing.

Cassava Yeast Rolls

I found this recipe in a Cuban-American cookbook and loved the nice nutty flavor of the rolls.

non-stick cooking spray

1 medium Cassava (Yucca) peeled and cut into small pieces

2 packets dry yeast

2 tbsp. sugar

2 tbsp. lukewarm water

1 cup milk

1 tsp. salt

4 tbsp. butter

3 ½ cups flour

1 large egg

1 tbsp. olive oil

Preheat the oven to 360° F (180° C).

Prepare two loaf pans by spraying lightly with cooking spray or greasing.

Boil the cassava in water until tender. Remove the cassava and place into a small bowl. Mash with a fork or potato masher until smooth. Set aside.

In a medium bowl dissolve the yeast with the sugar and lukewarm water. Cover and set aside until the mixture is bubbly.

In a small saucepan, over medium heat, add the milk, salt and butter stir until butter is melted. Remove the milk mixture from the heat and stir into the mashed cassava. Set aside.

In a large mixing bowl add 3 cups of flour. Make a well in the center and add the yeast mixture, the cassava mixture and the egg. Lightly combine all the ingredients together.

Turn the dough onto a floured surface and knead dough until soft and elastic, about 10 minutes. Transfer Dough to a large bowl, cover and leave for 1 hour, or until dough has doubled in size.

Punch down dough and divide into equal halves. Form halves into loaves and place into the prepared loaf pans. Brush the top of loaves lightly with olive oil. Cover and let rise for 25 minutes, or until doubled in size.

Place in oven and bake for 45 minutes. Check for doneness by tapping the bottom of loaves, it should sound hollow if it's done.

Remove from pan and cool lightly. Serve warm.

Then God said Let the land produce vegetation, seed-bearing plants and trees on the land that bear fruit with seed in it according to their various kinds.

Genesis 1:11

St Lucia S-Shaped Raisin Buns

Servings: 12 – 14 buns

¾ cup milk

⅓ cup sugar

2 tsp. salt

½ cup butter

1 packet dry yeast

½ cup warm water

1 tsp. ground cardamom

4 ⅓ cups sifted flour

1 egg

raisins

1 egg white

Pre-heat the oven to 375° F (190° C).

Heat milk and pour into a bowl. Add sugar, salt and butter. Cool to lukewarm.

Sprinkle yeast on warm water and stir to dissolve.

Add cardamom, 1 cup flour, yeast and egg to milk mixture. Beat with electric mixer at medium speed until smooth, about 3 minutes. Stir in enough remaining flour, a little at a time, until dough leaves the sides of bowl.

Turn onto lightly floured board and knead until smooth and elastic, about 5 minutes. Place in lightly greased bowl, turning to grease top. Cover and let rise until doubled, about 30 - 40 minutes. Punch down, cover, and let rest 10 minutes.

Pinch off balls of dough 2 ½" in diameter and roll into strips 12" long and ½" thick. Form into the shape of an S, coiling the ends. Place a few, about 3, raisins in the center of each coil.

Brush tops of buns with egg white beaten until foamy. Sprinkle with sugar. Cover and let rise until doubled, about 35 minutes.

Pre-heat the

Bake in pre-heated oven for 10 -15 minutes, or until golden.

Coconut Bun Tarts

These are still one of my favorite tarts. The spongy dough makes it's enjoyable to eat. A great snack time treat!

2 packets dry active yeast

2 tbsp. sugar

1 cup lukewarm water

3 cups all-purpose flour plus 1 cup for dusting

½ cup brown sugar

½ cup sugar

½ cup milk

1 tbsp. butter

1 tbsp. shortening

1 tsp. ground cinnamon

½ tsp. ground nutmeg

2 tbsp. water for brushing tops and edges

FILLING

3 cups grated coconut

1 cup sugar

2 tbsp. water

1 tsp. pear or almond extract

red food coloring

Make the filling in a medium saucepan on medium heat. Add coconut, sugar, water, extract and a few drops of food coloring and cook for 10 minutes. Remove from heat and cool.

Pre-heat the oven to 350° F (180° C).

Lightly grease 2 cookie sheets or spray with non-stick cooking spray.

In a medium bowl dissolve the yeast, sugar and warm water. Cover and set aside until bubbly.

In a large bowl add the flour, make a well in the center and add the sugars, milk, butter, shortening, spices and vanilla. Lightly combine all the ingredients together.

Turn dough out onto a lightly floured surface and knead to smooth and soft (but not sticky) dough. Cover with a towel and let rest for 30 minutes until doubled in size.

Remove the dough from the bowl and cut into pieces about the size of an orange. Form into balls, cover and rest for 30 minutes until doubled in size.

On a floured surface roll each ball into a thick circle about ¼" thick. Place a large spoonful of coconut mixture on one side of the circle, moisten the edges with some water and fold over to enclose filling, being careful that the coconut mixture does not come too close to the edges. Use a fork to crimp the edges closed. Place tarts on cookie sheets and leave for 20 minutes.

Brush tops with water and bake for 20 – 25 minutes, or until golden brown.

Remove from oven and cool.

Serve tarts warm.

Jamaica Fruit Buns

2 packets dry active yeast (about 2 oz. each)

¼ cup lukewarm water

6 cups all-purpose flour

1 ½ cups brown sugar

1 cup butter (2 sticks)

1 cup golden raisins

½ cup mixed peel

¼ cup glace cherries

2 eggs

1 tsp. vanilla extract

1 tsp. ground nutmeg

1 tsp. allspice

1 tsp. ground cinnamon

1 cup water

1 cup milk

1 tsp. salt

1 tbsp. golden syrup for glazing

Preheat the oven to 350° F (180° C).

Grease 2 medium round cake pans or lightly coat with non-stick cooking spray.

In a medium bowl place the yeast in the warm water, cover and let sit for 15 minutes, or until bubbly.

In a large bowl add the flour and make a well in the center.

Over medium heat the milk and water. Pour into a large bowl, add the butter, sugar, salt, eggs and spices and mix until combined. Add mixture to the flour along with the yeast and fruits. Mix well into a stiff dough. Place dough onto a lightly floured surface and knead well. Dough should not be sticky. Cover with a damp cloth and leave to rise for 30 minutes, or until doubled in size.

Turn dough out on a floured surface and punch back. Cut into two pieces. Roll each piece into a large disc and place into prepared cake pans. Cover and leave to rise until doubled in size, or reaches ¾ of the way to the top of the pans.

Bake in the oven for 25 minutes.

Remove buns from the oven and brush tops with the syrup. Return to the oven and bake for another 15 - 20 minutes.

Remove buns and place on wire racks to cool.

Serve warm.

Guadeloupe French Baguettes

This is a simple French baguette recipe. Due to the lack of fat it doesn't last and makes it difficult to be saved for another day. It's best eaten the same day it is baked and goes well served either as a lunch or dinner bread.

Servings: 1 loaf

1 packet active dry yeast

¼ cup warm water plus ½ cup

1 tsp. sugar

3 cups all-purpose flour plus extra flour for dusting

1 tsp. salt

Pre-heat the oven to 400° F (200° C).

In a small bowl combine the yeast and sugar with the water, stir to dissolve yeast and leave for 5 minutes, or until bubbly.

In a large mixing bowl add the flour and salt. Add the yeast mixture and the ½ cup water. Mix together adding extra water if needed until stiff dough forms. Turn dough onto a floured surface and knead dough until dough is smooth and satiny, about 5-10 minutes. Shape dough into a ball.

Place dough in a lightly greased bowl and turn to grease all the sides. Cover and place in a warm place to rise until doubled in size, about 1 hour.

Punch dough down, cover and let rise again in a warm place until doubled in size, about 1 hour.

Punch dough down again and cover and rest for 10 minutes.

Place dough on a floured surface and pat into a rectangular about 12" long.

Roll up jelly-roll fashion into a 12" long cylinder shape. Pinch ends and seam to seal. Place loaf on a lightly greased cookie or baking sheet with seam side down.

Cut 4 - 5 diagonal slashes with a sharp knife or razor blade. Cover dough loosely with a clean towel or plastic wrap and let rise in a warm place until doubled in size, about 45 minutes.

Place a shallow pan with boiling water on the bottom rack of the pre-heated oven.

Brush loaf lightly with water and place on the middle shelf of the oven.

Bake until the loaf is golden and sounds hollow when tapped on the bottom, about 30 minutes.

Remove loaf from the baking sheet and place on a wire rack to cool.

Guyanese Tennis Rolls

Servings: about 18 rolls

1 packet active dry yeast

¼ cup warm water (110° F)

¼ cup butter or margarine

1 cup sugar

1 tsp. salt

1 cup milk, scalded

2 whole eggs and 1 egg yolk beaten

1 egg white

1 tsp. grated lemon or orange zest

2 tsp. lemon extract

1 tsp. vanilla extract

4 ½ - 5 cups flour

Pre-heat the oven to 375° F (190° C).

Soften the yeast in warm water.

Add butter or margarine, sugar, salt, lemon zest, lemon extract and vanilla extract to the scalded milk. Let cool to lukewarm.

When cool, add yeast, eggs and enough flour to make a batter. Beat well. Add more flour, a little at a time, to make soft dough.

Turn onto a lightly floured surface and knead until satiny.

Brush oil on the top of dough while it proves the first time, this prevents it from getting crusty.

Place in a greased bowl, cover with a damp cloth and let rise until doubled in size. Punch down, shape into rolls and let rise again.

Make sure you have enough time to let the dough prove twice. The dough has to be soft, almost like a thick batter.

Brush with egg white mixed with water and bake for 25 to 30 minutes. Adjust oven temperature if necessary to get even baking and browning.

Corn Meal Bread

This Bread is found in some of the Spanish-speaking Caribbean; it has dense texture makes a great breakfast bread.

Servings: 1 Loaf.

½ cup cornmeal

1 tbsp. brown sugar

2 tsp. salt

2 tbsp. butter

1 ¼ cups hot milk

1 packet active yeast

4 cups flour plus extra for dusting work surface

Pre-heat the oven to 375° F (190° C).

In a large bowl, or the bowl of a stand mixer, add the cornmeal, sugar, salt and butter.

Add ¾ cup of the hot milk to the cornmeal mixture and mix together until combined.

Cool the remaining milk to lukewarm and add the yeast to the milk. Let the yeast mixture stand for 10 minutes.

Add the yeast mixture to the cornmeal mixture.

Add the flour to the cornmeal mixture, a little at a time, until firm dough is formed. Lightly flour the top of a flat surface and knead the dough until smooth and elastic. Place the dough in an oiled bowl, cover with a towel and let rise for an hour, until doubled in size.

Punch dough down, form into a loaf and place in a greased loaf pan to rise until almost doubled in size.

Bake for 45 minutes, or until golden. The bread should sound hollow when tapped on the bottom.

Remove loaf from the pan and cool on a rack before serving.

Cakes & Cookies

Christmas time in the Caribbean is the time of all round island fun and festivities. It's also the time where cakes and cookies are made in abundance from the traditional rum-soaked fruit cakes (which are made weeks in advance to give ample time for the rum-soaking process), local puddings and sweets, to the light and airy pound cakes. As with most youngsters in the Caribbean, my early cake baking career started by me scraping the leftover cake batter from the cake bowl. If I was lucky, I got enough scraped batter to put into a small buttered pan to make my own cake. And finished off by licking my fingers with what was left from the bowl!

Chef Freda

Island Folk Tale: The Rum Thief

There was once a man working in one of the rum factories; he found a great way for stealing his maker rum. When he got into work early in the morning, He always wears his coat. He removed his coat and placed it in the rum vats letting it sit all day.

When his shift was over, and he is getting ready to go home, he removed his coat and placed it in a plastic bag. At home, the coat is wrung out, and the prized rum is left to settle. This is then placed in a bottle and kept for drinking and sharing with friends.

Caribbean Rum Fruit Cake

Fruit cakes are made all over the islands of the Caribbean, especially during the holiday season. These rich golden are dark rum soaked cakes are loaded with dried fruits, nuts, and spices. Some are made weeks in advance, so there is ample time for the liquor soaking process. In preparation for the holiday season, dried fruits are soaked in rum months in advance to get them ready for these delicious rum heady cakes. Soak two weeks in advance in a tightly secured glass container.

2 cups golden raisins

1 cup currants

1 cup mixed candied fruits (cherries, pineapple)

½ cup mixed peel

¼ cup prunes (dried plums)

2 cups dark rum

1 cup cherry brandy

CAKE

3 ½ cups brown sugar

2 cups butter

6 eggs

¼ cup brown food coloring

1 ½ cup all-purpose flour

1 tsp. baking powder

1 tsp. ground cinnamon

½ tsp. ground nutmeg

½ tsp. ground allspice

¼ tsp. ground cloves

1 tsp. vanilla extract

Preheat oven to 350° F (180° C).

Grease 2 round cake pans, dust lightly with flour and shake off excess.

Cream the butter and sugar together until combined, about 15 minutes.

Add eggs one at a time, beating after each addition.

Add the soaked fruit with half of the liquid. Add the food coloring, a little at a time, until you have the desired depth of color. Stir well.

Add sifted flour, baking powder and spices. Add vanilla extract and mix the mixture lightly until completely combined.

Pour mixture into prepared baking pans.

Bake the cakes at 350° F (180° C) for about 2 hours.

Remove cake from oven when done and brush leftover rum mixture on the top of the cake; this can be done every few hours.

Leave the cakes in pans for 1 - 2 days before serving.

Banana Spice Cake

This rich, moist cake gives off a heavenly smell. With the abundance of bananas all over the islands, this is a sure treat not to be missed.

3 very ripe bananas, mashed

½ cup butter, softened

2 tbsp. milk

2 eggs

1 cup sugar

1 tsp. vanilla extract

1 ½ cups all-purpose flour

1 tsp. baking powder

½ tsp. baking soda

1 tsp. ground cinnamon

1 tsp. ground nutmeg

½ tsp. ground allspice

RUM GLAZE

¼ cup rum

½ cup sweetened condensed milk

1 tbsp. butter

2 tbsp. orange juice

To make glaze combine all ingredients in a small saucepan and boil for 5 minutes

Preheat oven to 350° F (180° C).

Lightly grease 2 square cake pans, dust lightly with flour and shake off excess. A light coat of cooking spray can also be used.

In a large bowl blend the bananas, butter, milk, eggs, sugar and vanilla extract.

Mix together the flour, baking powder, baking soda and spices. Combine into the banana mixture and mix lightly.

Pour batter into the prepared cake pans.

Bake the cakes for 45 minutes, or until cake leaves the side of pan.

Remove from the oven and pour rum glaze on the top while cake is still warm. Let cakes set for 15 minutes.

Serve warm.

Did you know? Caribbean Banana Facts

Banana trees can be found on almost all of the islands of the Caribbean and most islanders will have a banana tree planted in their backyard or right along with the flower beds. Up to the 1980's, banana export was a major revenue earner on most of the islands, most notably on the islands of Dominica, Saint Lucia, Grenada, Trinidad and St Vincent. However, with the development of tourism, banana no longer plays the important role as the main island export and is now only cultivated for local consumption. Nowadays, lands which were once cultivated with banana plantations, are now dotted with resorts and inns.

Jamaica Toto Spice Coconut Cake

3 cups all-purpose flour

1 ½ cups brown sugar

1 ½ cups desiccated (unsweetened) or freshly grated coconut

3 tsp. baking powder

1 tsp. baking soda

½ tsp. allspice

½ tsp. nutmeg

1 tsp. ground ginger

½ tsp. salt

½ cup raisins

¼ cup dried cherries or cranberries

2 eggs, well beaten

2 cups milk

½ cup butter, melted

1 tsp. vanilla extract

1 tbsp. Jamaican rum

Preheat oven to 350° F (180° C).

In a large bowl mix together all the dry ingredients.

Beat eggs and milk together and add melted butter. Add vanilla and rum.

Add liquid to the bowl with dry ingredients and mix until blended. Do not over mix.

Place batter in a greased square or loaf baking pan (about 13□ x 8□).

Bake the cake for 1 hour.

Cool, in the baking dish, on rack before cutting into squares and serving.

Chocolate Mango Cheesecake Cupcakes

FOR THE CUPCAKES

2 cups (1 12oz. packet) semi-sweet chocolate chips, divided

1 ½ cups all-purpose flour

1 tsp. baking soda

½ tsp. salt

½ cup granulated sugar

⅓ cup vegetable oil

1 large egg

1 tsp. vanilla extract

1 cup water

MANGO CHEESECAKE FILLING

6 oz. cream cheese, room temperature

½ tbsp. cornstarch (dissolved in a teaspoon of water)

¼ cup granulated sugar

½ cup pureed mango

1 large egg

⅛ tsp. salt

DIRECTIONS FOR THE CUPCAKES

Preheat the oven to 350° F (180° C).

Line two standard muffin tins with 16 paper liners.

Place ½ cup of the chocolate chips in a small microwave-safe bowl and microwave on high for 45 seconds. Stir until smooth. If not completely melted return to the microwave for 10-second bursts until smooth. Let cool.

In a medium bowl combine the flour, baking soda and salt.

In a large bowl vigorously whisk the sugar, oil, egg and vanilla until well combined. Beat in the melted chocolate chips. Gradually add the flour mixture alternatively with the water. The batter will be thin.

DIRECTIONS FOR THE FILLING

In the bowl of an electric mixer beat the cream cheese, cornstarch mixture, sugar, mango puree, egg and salt until creamy.

Fill each muffin cup ½ full with the chocolate batter. Spoon a tablespoon of the mango cream cheese filling over the batter. Spoon the remaining batter over the cream cheese filling.

Bake for 20 to 25 minutes, or until a cake tester inserted in the center comes out clean.

While still hot sprinkle the remaining ½ cup chocolate chips onto the cupcakes.

Let cool for 5 minutes, or until the chocolate chips are shiny and then spread to frost.

Cool completely on a wire rack.

Cooking is like love; it should be entered into with abandon or not at all.

Harriet Van Horne

Golden Rum Cake

This is an allspice pound cake speckled with some island rum.

1 ½ cups butter

1 ½ cups sugar

1 tsp. vanilla extract

4 eggs

1 tbsp. grated orange zest

½ cup dark rum

1 cup pineapple juice

3 cups all-purpose flour

1 ½ tsp. baking powder

½ tsp. baking soda

½ cup evaporated milk

Preheat the oven to 350° F (180° C).

Prepare 2 round cake pans by lightly greasing with butter or cooking spray and dust lightly with flour.

Cream together the butter and sugar until light and fluffy. Add the vanilla extract and eggs one at a time, beating lightly after each addition. Add the orange rind, rum, and juice.

Combine the flour, baking powder and baking soda. Add to the butter mixture alternately with the milk until combined. Pour batter into prepared pans.

Bake for 45 minutes to 1 hour, or a knife inserted in the center comes out clean. Cool.

Serve warm.

Chewy Banana Oatmeal Cookies

¾ cup salted butter

1 cup brown sugar, packed

½ cup granulated sugar

1 egg

1 tsp. vanilla extract

1 cup mashed banana

1 ½ cups flour

1 ½ tsp. ground cinnamon

1 tsp. ground ginger

1 tsp. baking soda

1/4 tsp. ground cloves

2 tsp. cornstarch

3 cups old fashioned oats

¼ cup dried fruit (cherries and/or raisins)

¼ cup powder sugar for dusting

Preheat oven to 350° F (180° C).

Mix together butter, brown sugar, granulated sugar, egg, vanilla extract and mashed bananas until well combined.

Add flour, cinnamon, ginger, baking soda, cloves and cornstarch and mix until combined.

Stir in oats and dried fruits.

Spoon a tablespoon of dough onto a cookie sheet covered with parchment paper. Flatten dough, a little bit, into thick discs. They will spread a little when baked.

Bake for 10 - 12 minutes, or until edges just starts to golden.

Remove from oven and cool on the cookie sheet for 3 - 4 minutes and then move to a cooling rack to cool completely.

Dust with sifted powder sugar.

Baking Tip

To prevent parchment paper from slipping off baking sheets sprinkle the baking sheets with a few drops of water before placing sheets on the pan.

Chef Freda

Spiced Pumpkin Cheesecake

CRUST

1 ¼ cups Shirley Biscuit or Graham Cracker crumbs (10 biscuits/crackers)

¼ cup sugar

4 tbsp. unsalted butter, melted

FILLING

4 packets (8 oz. each) bar cream cheese, very soft

1 ¼ cups sugar

3 tbsp. all-purpose flour

1 cup cooked mashed pumpkin, drain to remove excess liquid (or use canned pure pumpkin puree)

1 tbsp. pumpkin pie spice (or substitute with 1 tsp. ground cinnamon, 1 tsp. ground ginger ½ tsp. ground cloves and ½ tsp. ground nutmeg)

1 tbsp. vanilla extract

½ tsp. salt

4 large eggs at room temperature

Preheat oven to 350° F (180° C) with the rack in center.

Assemble a 9-inch non-stick spring form pan, with the raised side of the bottom part facing up.

Add the biscuits/crackers in a food processor and pulse until it resembles fine crumbs. This can also be done by rolling in a towel with a bottle or rolling pin. In a medium bowl mix cracker crumbs, sugar and butter until moistened. Press firmly into bottom of pan.

Bake until golden around edges, 10 to 12 minutes.

FILLING

With an electric mixer beat cream cheese and sugar on low speed until smooth and then mix in flour. Do not overmix. Add pumpkin puree, pie spice, vanilla and salt and mix just until smooth. Add eggs one at a time, mixing until each is incorporated before adding the next.

Place spring form pan on a rimmed baking sheet. Pour filling into spring form and gently smooth top. Transfer to oven and reduce the oven to 300° F (150° C).

Bake for 45 minutes. Turn off the oven and leave the cheesecake in the oven another 2 hours more. Do not open the oven.

Remove from oven and let cool completely.

Cover with plastic wrap and refrigerate until firm, at least 2 - 4 hours. Remove from mold before serving.

Serve with whipped cream.

Freda's Carrot Cake with Cream Cheese Frosting

I enjoy making carrot cake, and I have experimented with lots of recipes. In this recipe (which was adaptive from the silver palate cookbook), I cook the carrots instead of traditionally grating them. The result is a rich cake/ pudding like texture that's sure to please any palate.

Chef Freda

Servings: 14

3 eggs

1 cup sugar

1 cup brown sugar

1 ½ cups vegetable oil

2 tsp. vanilla extract

1 can crushed pineapples (17 oz.)

2 cups cooked carrots, pureed

1 cup coconut flakes

3 cups all-purpose flour

1 tsp. baking powder

1 tsp. baking soda

1 tsp. allspice

1 tsp. ground cinnamon

1 tsp. ground nutmeg

½ tsp. salt

1 cup chopped walnuts

Preheat oven to 350° F (180° C).

Lightly grease and flour a bundt cake pan, or other pan of choice.

In a large mixing bowl cream the eggs, sugars and oil together.

Add the vanilla, pineapple, carrots and coconut, Mix the dry ingredients together and add the dry ingredients into the batter, a little at a time. Fold in the nuts.

Pour the batter into the prepared pans.

Bake in the oven for 1 hour, or done. Check for doneness by inserting knife in the center and if the knife comes out clean, it's done.

Serve warm lightly dusted with powdered sugar.

Cream Cheese Frosting

8 oz. cream cheese

½ cup butter

1 box (16oz.) of confectioners' sugar (about 4 cups)

1 tbsp. banana liqueur

1 cup toasted coconut

In a medium bowl, or mixer, beat the cream cheese and butter until light. Add the powder sugar, a little at a time. Stir in the banana liqueur. Beat until light and fluffy.

Frost the top and sides of cake.

Sprinkle with toasted coconut flakes to finish.

Chill the cake to set, or until ready to serve.

Serve sliced.

Coconut Cream Cake

This cake takes a little more time to make because of the delicious coconut frosting. However, it's worth the extra effort.

1 cup butter

1 cup sugar

1 cup grated fresh coconut

1 ¾ cups all-purpose flour

4 tsp. baking powder

1 cup coconut water (or substitute with milk)

1 tsp. coconut or rum extract

4 egg whites

Preheat oven to 350° F (180° C).

Grease two 9" cake pans.

Cream the butter and sugar together until light and fluffy. Add grated coconut.

Sift flour and baking powder together and add to creamed mixture, alternating with the coconut water.

Beat egg whites until soft peaks form and fold lightly into the batter. Pour into prepared pans.

Bake for 20 - 25 minutes.

Remove from oven to cool.

Place on a large serving platter and frost layers with Coconut Frosting (next recipe).

Coconut Frosting

1 cup sugar

⅓ cup boiling water

¼ cup cream of tartar

1 tsp. light corn syrup

2 egg whites

1 tsp. coconut or rum extract

2 cups grated coconut

In a double boiler mix sugar, water, cream of tartar and corn syrup. This can also be done by bringing a large pot of water to boil and setting a stainless bowl on the top of pot. The bowl must not touch the water.

Stir until sugar dissolves. Add the egg whites and remove from heat. Beat the mixture on high speed for 5 minutes.

Return pan to heat. Keep the water on a low simmer and heat mixture for another 3 minutes.

Add the coconut extract and beat until glossy and spreadable, 3 to 5 minutes.

Frost the layers of the cake and stack both layers on top of each other.

Frost sides and top of cake and sprinkle with grated coconut flakes.

Chill until firm, about 1 hour.

Guavas: Did you know?

Guavas grow wild all over the Caribbean. The tree which is very bushy bears a small white flower. The fruit start as small green berries, which grows into a round thin skin fruit that turns a bright yellow when the Fruit is ripe and ready for picking. Depending on the variety the inside flesh of the fruit can be pink, white, yellow or bright red. Guavas are eaten on their own or prepared in jams, jellies, drinks, cheeses; they are also used to flavor cakes, pies, ice cream, and sauces. In the following recipe, I used frozen guava pulp and guava nectar found in specialty food store or Caribbean markets

Chef Freda

Guava Cake

2 cups sugar

1 cup butter

4 eggs

3 cups all-purpose flour

1 tsp. baking powder

½ tsp. baking soda

1 tsp. ground cinnamon

½ tsp. ground nutmeg

1 cup frozen guava puree

½ cup guava nectar

Preheat the oven to 350° F (180° C).

Grease and flour a 2-inch cake pan.

Cream the sugar and butter together until light and fluffy. Add eggs one at a time, beating after each addition.

Sift dry ingredients together.

In a small bowl, mix together the guava puree and guava nectar. Fold dry ingredients into the butter mixture, alternating with the juice until blended. Pour into prepared pan.

Bake the cake for 30 minutes, or until cake leaves the side of pan.

Cool cake, remove from pan and frost with rum buttercream.

Rum Buttercream Frosting

1 cup butter softened

3 cups powdered sugar

3 tbsp. dark rum

5 tbsp. whipping cream

1 tsp. vanilla extract

Combine butter, powdered sugar, rum and whipping cream.

Beat with a mixer until light and creamy.

Stir in vanilla extract.

Add extra powdered sugar if needed.

Bakers Biscuits

Caribbean cookies are known as biscuits and were normally made using leftover ingredients. I got this recipe from an old baking pal Eddy, who used to make it using leftover flour and shortening after his morning baking. In this recipe, I have replaced some of the shortenings with butter. It's quick and easy to make and has the texture of an English shortbread.

Chef Freda

2 cups all-purpose flour

pinch of salt

½ cup butter (1 stick)

½ cup vegetable shortening

½ cup sugar

½ tsp. cinnamon

½ tsp. ground nutmeg

½ tsp. ground ginger

Preheat the oven to 300° F (150° C).

Grease a cookie sheet and lightly dust with flour, shaking off excess. Cream butter and shortening with sugar in a mixer until light and creamy.

Sift flour and salt with spices. Mix flour into butter mixture and combine.

Gather dough into a ball, wrap in plastic wrap and chill for about 1 hour (I found this makes it easier to work with the dough when rolling it out).

Roll dough out on a floured surface and cut into desired shapes. Gather scraps form into a ball and re-roll.

Place on prepared sheets and bake until light brown.

VARIATION: Coconut Bakers Biscuits

Add ½ cup shredded coconut to the mixture.

When baking follow directions; when cooking go by your own taste.

Laiko Bahrs

Caribbean Ginger Snap

Ginger is grown on most of the islands and used in all manner of cooking by the locals. The ginger available on some of the islands, have smaller roots or rhizomes compared to the larger ginger rhizomes that are found in most major supermarkets. I personally prefer the smaller roots since I find them to have a stronger ginger taste. Caribbean Ginger is used in teas, sauces, cakes, breads, and cookies. Gingersnaps are one of my favorite cookies and a great way to use fresh ginger for a real tropical ginger flavor.

½ cup butter

¼ vegetable shortening

¼ cup molasses 1 cup sugar

1 egg beaten

1 tbsp. ginger juice, (grate and squeeze a large ginger stem, about 4oz.)

2 cups all-purpose flour

2 tsp. baking powder

1 tsp. ground ginger

1 tsp. cinnamon

1 tsp. ground cloves

brown sugar for dipping

Preheat oven to 350° F (180° C).

Grease and lightly flour 2 cookie sheets.

Cream butter, shortening, and sugar together. Add molasses, egg and ginger juice, beating well to combine.

Sift the dry ingredients together and add to the butter mixture.

Place dough in a bowl, cover and chill for up to 1 hour.

Remove dough and form into small golf-sized balls.

Dip in brown sugar and place on sheets, leaving enough space between cookies to prevent sticking.

Bake for 10 - 12 minutes.

Serve warm or store in airtight container to keep them crispy.

Puerto Rico's Sweet Potato Cake

I found this unique recipe for sweet potato cake in an old Puerto Rican cookbook. After adjusting some of the ingredients and adding some of the island spices to result turned out to be a wonderful tasting cake.

Chef Freda

1 ½ lb. sweet potato (about 3 large sweet potatoes)

1 medium pot of boiling water

pinch of salt

1 ½ cups butter

8 eggs

2 ½ cups sugar

1 tsp. ground cinnamon

1 tsp. ground nutmeg

1 tsp. vanilla extract

1 cup all-purpose flour

2 cups warm milk

Preheat the oven to 350° F (180° C).

Lightly spray a bandit cake pan with some vegetable spray, dust lightly with flour and shake off excess.

Scrub sweet potatoes and cut into small pieces. Place in the pot of salted water and bring to a boil. Boil until potatoes are soft. Remove potatoes and drain to remove excess water. Remove skin and mash with a vegetable ricer.

Melt butter in a medium pan. Add the potato, butter and eggs, one at a time mixing after each addition. Mix in sugar, cinnamon, nutmeg and vanilla extract.

In a medium bowl mix the flour with the warm milk, mixing thoroughly to dissolve the flour. Add the flour mixture to the potato mixture. Mix batter to combine thoroughly. Pour batter into prepared pan.

Bake the cake for 2 ½ hours.

Remove cake and cool completely.

Place on a serving platter and dust with powdered sugar to serve.

Caribbean Lime Pound Cake

Nothing beats a slice of rich buttery pound cake, and with the addition of the lime, it gives a kick to this tropical flavored pound cake recipe.

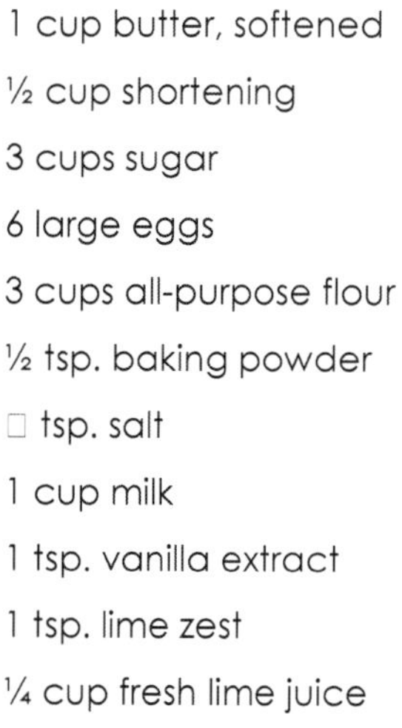

1 cup butter, softened

½ cup shortening

3 cups sugar

6 large eggs

3 cups all-purpose flour

½ tsp. baking powder

□ tsp. salt

1 cup milk

1 tsp. vanilla extract

1 tsp. lime zest

¼ cup fresh lime juice

Preheat oven to 325° F (160° C).

Beat butter and shortening at medium speed with a heavy-duty electric stand mixer until creamy. Gradually add sugar, beating at medium speed until light and fluffy. Add eggs one at a time, beating until just blended after each addition.

Stir together flour, baking powder and salt. Add to butter mixture alternately with milk, beginning and ending with flour mixture. Beat at low speed just until blended after each addition. Stir in vanilla, lime zest and lime juice. Pour batter into a greased and floured 10" (12-cup) tube pan.

Bake the cake for 1 hour and 15 minutes to 1 hour and 20 minutes, or until a long wooden pick inserted in center comes out clean.

Cool in the pan on a wire rack for 10 to 15 minutes and remove from the pan to the wire rack. Prepare the Lime Rum Glaze whilst the cake cools.

Immediately brush the top and sides of cake with Lime Rum Glaze.

Cool completely for about 1 hour.

Slice and Serve.

Lime Rum Glaze

1 cup powdered sugar

1 tbsp. fresh key lime juice

½ tsp. dark rum

Whisk together powdered sugar, fresh key lime juice and rum until smooth. Use the glaze immediately.

My idea of Heaven is a great big baked potato and someone to share it with.

Oprah Winfrey

Nassau Rum Cake

3 ½ cups all-Purpose Flour

½ tsp. baking powder

½ tsp. baking soda

¾ tsp. salt

¼ tsp. nutmeg

¼ tsp. cinnamon

1 ½ cup unsalted butter, softened

2 cups granulated sugar

4 large eggs

2 egg yolks

1 tbsp. vanilla extract

¾ cup coconut milk (canned)

Preheat your oven to 350° F (180° C).

Spray a bundt pan with baking spray, dust with flour and shake off excess.

In a medium bowl sift together the flour, baking powder, baking soda, salt, nutmeg and cinnamon. Set aside.

In the bowl of your stand-mixer beat together the butter and sugars until light and fluffy, approximately 15 -20 minutes.

In a small bowl beat together the eggs, egg yolks and vanilla. Slowly pour the mixture into the creamed butter, scraping the sides as needed. After the eggs are completely incorporated, gently stir in ⅓ of the flour mixture, and then about half of the coconut milk.

Mix in another 1/3 of the flour mixture, the rest of the coconut milk and the remaining ⅓ of the flour until just combined. Pour the batter into the prepared bundt pan.

Bake the cake for 55 to 60 minutes, or until done. Check for doneness by inserting a wooden skewer into the center of the cake. If it comes out clean it's done.

Remove cake from oven and while still hot generously poke holes in the cake with a bamboo (wooden) skewer. Spoon the Coconut Rum Syrup over the cake, allowing the syrup to soak into the cake. Note: start making the syrup when the cake is almost done baking.

Leave the cake in the pan to completely cool and absorb the syrup.

Once the cake is cool invert it onto a serving platter. Brush off any remaining syrup from the top of the cake and serve.

OPTIONAL

Finish with the Coconut Glaze (recipe below).

Coconut Rum Syrup

¾ cup canned coconut milk

6 tbsp. sugar

½ cup dark Bahaman rum (any brand will work)

In a medium saucepan over medium heat warm the coconut milk and the sugar, stirring until the sugar dissolves. It shouldn't come to a boil.

Remove the syrup from heat and add the dark rum. Whisk everything together.

Set aside until the cake comes out of the oven.

Coconut Glaze

4 tbsp. butter, diced

6 tbsp. heavy cream

6 tbsp. brown sugar

pinch of salt

1 tbsp. dark rum

½ cup sweetened coconut flakes, toasted

Toast the coconut flakes on the cookie sheet. Keep a careful watch to prevent burning. Toss them around as they are toasting.

Once they are golden, remove from the oven and set aside.

Combine the butter, cream, salt and sugar together in a small saucepan over high heat and bring to a boil. Stir the mixture to dissolve the sugar; this should take about 90 seconds.

Remove from the heat, whisk in the rum and let cool completely.

Once the syrup has cooled whisk in the toasted coconut.

You have to go out on a limb sometimes because that's where the fruit is.

Will Rogers

Chocolate, Coconut & Guava Filled Swiss Roll

Servings: 8

CAKE

3 eggs

1/3 cup sugar

1/3 cup self-rising flour

1 tbsp. Coco Lopez

¼ cup grated coconut

6 tbsp. guava jelly

CHOCOLATE FROSTING

7 oz. semi-sweet chocolate

5 tbsp. butter

2 tbsp. light corn syrup

Preheat the oven to 350° F (180° C).

Grease and line with parchment paper a 9 x 12" jelly roll pan.

With an electric mixer in a medium bowl beat the eggs and sugar until light and foamy, about 10 minutes.

Sift the flour and fold into the egg mixture with a spatula or spoon. Fold in the Coco Lopez and grated coconut.

Pour into the prepared pan and level off.

Bake in the oven for 10 - 15 minutes, or until springy to the touch

Sprinkle a sheet of parchment with a little sugar and place on top of a damp dish towel. Turn the cake out onto the paper and carefully peel away the parchment lining.

Spread the guava jelly over the sponge and roll up from the short ends using the dish towel to help with the rolling.

Place the jelly roll seam side down on a wire rack to cool.

TO MAKE THE FROSTING

Melt the chocolate and butter together, stirring to combine.

Add the syrup and stir. Let the mixture cool for 5 minutes.

Spread the mixture over the jelly roll and leave until the frosting sets.

Cut the Swiss roll into slices and serve with fresh fruit.

Everyone is kneaded out of the same dough but not baked in the same oven.

Yiddish Proverb

Caribbean Spice Cake

Servings: 8 - 9

2 cups all-purpose Flour

1/½ tsp. ground cinnamon

1 tsp. baking powder

½ tsp. ground ginger

¼ tsp. ground nutmeg

¼ tsp. ground allspice

½ tsp. salt

½ cup margarine or butter softened (1 stick)

¼ cup sugar

1 cup brown sugar

2 large eggs

1 cup pineapple juice

½ cup raisins

Preheat the oven to 350° F (180° C).

Grease and lightly flour a round or square 9-inch cake pan.

Sift flour, cinnamon, baking powder, baking soda, ginger, nutmeg allspice and salt in a medium bowl.

In a mixer bowl or large bowl, cream together at low speed the margarine and both sugars until blended.

Increase the speed to medium and beat the mixture until light and fluffy, about 5 minutes.

Add the eggs one at a time, beating well after each addition. Reduce speed to low, add the pineapple juice and beat lightly.

Beat in the flour mixture until smooth, scraping down the sides. Stir in the raisins. Pour the batter into the prepared pan, spread evenly.

Bake the cake for 35 - 40 minutes, or until a toothpick inserted in the center comes out clean.

Cool completely in pan before removing the cake.

Jamaican Christmas Cake

Every Caribbean island I have ever visited has its own variation of Christmas cake. I have had the pleasure of sampling quite a few over the years, and they have all had some unique differences both in flavors and textures. The Christmas cake found in Jamaica is a bit heavier both in texture and the heady addition of the local rum. A great palate pleasure hands down!

Chef Freda

2 cups raisins

1 cup currants

1 cup prunes

½ cup cherries

½ cup mixed peel

2 cups dark rum

6 cups port wine

1 ½ cups dark brown sugar

1 cup all-purpose flour

1 cup dry breadcrumbs

1 tsp. baking powder

½ tsp. salt

1 tsp. ground cinnamon

1 tsp. grated nutmeg

1 cup butter

6 large eggs

½ cup chopped walnuts

1 tsp. orange or lime zest, finely chopped

1 tsp. vanilla extract

Chop or mince all the dried fruits and add to an airtight container. Add the rum and 4 cups of port wine cover tightly and soak for 2 - 3 weeks. Before using the soaked dried fruits simmer in the remaining port, cool and add.

Make the dark coloring for the cake by browning ¼ cup of the sugar over low heat until very dark, but not burnt.

Combine the flour, breadcrumbs, baking powder, salt and spices.

Cream the butter and remaining sugar together until light and fluffy. Add the eggs one at a time, mixing well until combined before adding the next egg. Add the cooled fruits, dark coloring and mix in the flour mixture. Add the nuts and orange zest. Pour into prepared baking pans.

Bake in the pre-heated oven at 350° F (180° C) for 1 ½ hours and then reduce the heat 300° F (150° C) and bake for another 15 minutes.

Cake is done when knife inserted in the center comes out clean.

Pineapple Upside-Down Cake

This is a classic pineapple upside down cake. The pineapple slices can also be substituted with mango slices.

Servings: 8 - 10

2 cans (8 oz. each) pineapple slices in juice

⅓ cup packed brown sugar

1 stick butter or margarine (4oz. / 8 tbsp.)

1 cup all-purpose flour

1 tsp. baking powder

¼ tsp. salt

½ tsp. ground cinnamon

⅔ cup sugar

2 medium eggs

1 tsp. almond extract

⅓ cup pineapple juice

8 glace cherries

Preheat the oven to 350° F (180° C).

Drain the pineapple and reserve ⅓ cup of the pineapple juice plus 2 tbsp.

Grease a 9" round cake pan and lightly dust with flour.

In a medium skillet over medium heat add brown sugar and 2 tbsp. butter and cook until melted. Stir in reserved 2 tbsp. pineapple juice and bring to a slow boil for 1 minute.

Pour mixture into the bottom of the cake pan making sure that the bottom is evenly covered with the mixture.

Place the pineapple slices in a circle in the pan on top of the sugar mixture. Make sure the slices fix snugly and lie flat. Place 1 glace cherry in the middle of each pineapple circle. Set aside.

In a medium bowl sift together the flour, baking powder, salt and cinnamon. In a large mixing bowl or mixer at high speed, beat the remaining butter and sugar until light and fluffy. Add the eggs one at a time and beat after each addition. Add the almond extract and stir in to blend. Add the flour mixture to the egg mixture alternately with the pineapple juice and beat lightly until the mixture is fully combined. Spoon the batter over the pineapples and spread evenly to cover.

Bake cake for 40 - 45 minutes, or until toothpick inserted into the center of the cake comes out clean.

Remove cake from the oven and run a thin knife around the cake to loosen from the sides off the pan.

Invert cake onto a serving plate.

Haitian Gateau De Patate

While living and working in South Florida, some of my dearest friends were of Haitian decedent. Haitians are known to be loving and sharing people, and it was always a joy during the holiday season to enjoy some of the Haitians culinary treats. One such treat is the Gateau De Patate, which has an almost pudding-like texture. It is normally served with a coconut cream sauce or Coquimol. But I find it also delicious eating it on its own.

Chef Freda

¼ cup softened butter

2 lb. sweet potatoes, peeled and cut into small pieces

1 large very ripe banana

3 eggs

1 cup sugar

⅓ cup dark corn syrup

¼ cup coconut milk

¼ cup evaporated milk

1 tsp. vanilla extract

1 tsp. ground cinnamon

1 tsp. grated nutmeg

¼ cup golden raisins

Preheat the oven to 350° F (180° C).

Prepare a round cake pan by spreading with 2 tbsp. of the softened butter.

Boil the potatoes in salted water until soft and drain well. Mash potato lightly with a fork.

In a mixing bowl beat the potato together with the banana. Add all the other ingredients and mix well. Pour the mixture into the prepared cake pan.

Bake the cake for 1 ½ hours.

Allow to cool and serve with Coquimol (coconut cream sauce).

Coquimol (Coconut Cream sauce)

¾ cup sugar

¾ cup water

1 ½ cups coconut cream (or use canned coconut milk)

6 egg yolks

2 tbsp. light rum

1 tsp. vanilla extract

1 pinch nutmeg

Boil the sugar and water over medium heat, stirring lightly, to dissolve sugar. Increase the heat and cook on high heat until the mixture turns into a syrup or softball stage.

Remove the pan from the heat and lightly stir in the coconut cream. Be careful with the steam from the hot liquid.

Mix the egg yolks in a medium bowl until combined. Add a small portion to the coconut mixture to temper. Slowly add the egg mixture to the rest of the coconut mixture and return to the heat. Reduce heat to low and cook over low heat for 3- 4 minutes until mixture resembles heavy cream.

Add the rum and vanilla and serve over the cake sprinkled with the nutmeg.

Pineapple Macaroon Cookies

Servings: 24 cookies.

1 whole small pineapple, peeled, cored and finely chopped (or a 14 oz. can sliced pineapple)

3 medium egg whites

1 cup sugar

2 ½ cups coconut flakes

12 candied cherries

Preheat the oven to 325° F (160° C).

Lightly grease, or line with parchment paper, two cookie sheets.

Drain the pineapple with a strainer to remove as much of the pineapple liquid as possible.

Beat the egg whites until they form stiff peaks. Gradually beat in the sugar, a little at a time.

Fold in the chopped pineapple and coconut flakes until combined. Be careful not to over mix.

Drop a spoonful of the cookie dough on the prepared sheet, piling to form cone-like shape. Leave enough space between each cookie to allow them to spread during baking.

Cut the cherries in half and place a half on top of each cookie.

Bake until brown and crisp about, 20 - 30 minutes.

Remove from oven and let cookies cool on the baking sheets.

Carefully remove cookies. Use a spatula to help.

Serve or store cookies in an airtight container until ready to use.

Cassava Biscuits

1 lb. sweet cassava or yucca, peeled and grated (wrap in cheese cloth and squeeze out juice to make 2 cups)

¼ cup butter

¼ cup vegetable shortening

½ cup sugar

1 egg

1 ½ cup grated fresh coconut

2 cups flour

1 tsp. baking powder

1 tsp. coconut extract

Preheat the oven to 375° F (190° C).

Lightly grease 2 large cookie sheets or line with parchment paper.

In a mixing bowl cream together the sugar, butter and shortening until the mixture is light and fluffy. Beat the egg lightly in a small bowl and add to the butter mixture along with the coconut and cassava.

Mix the flour and baking powder together. Fold a little at a time into the cream mixture until the mixture forms stiff dough. Using your hands add some more flour until a stiff dough is formed.

Place dough onto a lightly floured surface and knead with heels of hands for 2 - 3 minutes. Place finished dough on a flat, lightly floured surface and roll out into a medium thick circle. Using a cookie cutter cut into desired shapes. Gather scraps fold into ball roll out again and into more shapes. Place cookies 1 inch apart on prepared sheets.

Bake cookies for 20 minutes, or until golden.

Serve warm.

Murita's Dark Chocolate Cake with Chocolate Buttercream Frosting

My oldest daughter, Murita, is a die-hard chocolate cake lover and even though chocolate cakes are not a Caribbean cake specialty. I would be amiss if I did not include a chocolate cake recipe for her enjoyment. To add a touch of tropical Caribbean flavor to this delicious cake, I have topped it with a creamy St Martin's guava berry liqueur buttercream. Here to you Murita!

Chef Freda

1 ½ cups sugar

1 ¼ cup all-purpose flour

¾ cup unsweetened cocoa powder

2 ½ tsp. baking powder

1 ½ tsp. baking soda

1 cup evaporated milk

3 large eggs

2 tsp. vanilla extract

6 tbsp. cocoa powder

¾ cup hot coffee

¼ cup coffee liqueur

Preheat the oven to 350° F (180° C).

Lightly grease and flour three 8" round cake pans, shaking off excess flour.

In a large bowl mix together the sugar, flour, cocoa powder, baking powder, baking soda and salt.

In a small bowl lightly mix the eggs, milk and vanilla together until combined.

In a small saucepan over medium heat melt the butter with the coffee and liqueur.

In a large mixing bowl combine the flour mixture with half of the egg mixture and mix lightly. Add the coffee mixture and the remaining egg mixture. Scrape the sides of the bowl and mix into a smooth batter, being careful not over mix.

Pour batter into prepared pans.

Bake the cake for 20 - 30 minutes, or until cake pulls from the sides of the pan or is springy to the touch.

Cool cake in pan for 5 minutes. Remove cake and cool completely.

Frost cake middle, sides and top with Chocolate Buttercream Frosting.

Chocolate Buttercream Frosting

1 cup butter softened

¼ tsp. salt

3 cups powdered sugar

¼ cup whipping cream

1 tsp. vanilla

2 tbsp. cocoa powder

2 tbsp. crème de cacao

Combine butter, salt, powdered sugar, whipping cream, cocoa and cream de cocoa.

Beat mixture with an electric mixer or with a hand whisk until very smooth and creamy. Adjust consistency by adding more powdered sugar if needed or desired.

Guava and Pineapple Shortcake Sandwich

Servings: 12

1 ½ sticks butter (¾ cup), softened

⅓ cup sugar

1 egg

1 tsp. vanilla extract

2 cups self-rising flour

½ cup cornstarch

1 tsp. ground cinnamon

½ tsp. ground nutmeg

FILLING

½ cup diced pineapple

⅓ cup guava jam (or you can use pineapple jam)

Lightly grease a 9" removable bottom pan.

Make the filling by cooking the pineapple in 1 tbsp. of water until the fruit is soft. Add the guava jam, combine and leave to cool.

Beat the butter and sugar until light and fluffy. Beat in the egg and vanilla.

Sift the flour, cornstarch, cinnamon and nutmeg together.

Add the flour mixture to butter mixture and beat lightly to combine and form soft dough.

Divide the dough in half and roll out one piece on a floured surface to fit the bottom of the pan. Prick the dough with a fork and spread the fruit mixture on the top of the dough, being careful not get the fruit to close to the edge of the pan.

Dampen the edges with water.

Roll out the remaining half of the dough and place on top and lightly press in place to secure to the bottom. Evenly cover with the fruit.

Place in the refrigerator and chill for 30 minutes.

Preheat the oven to 350° F (180° C).

Bake the shortbread in the middle of the oven for 35 - 40 minutes, or until golden.

Allow to cool in pan before removing from the pan.

When cool and cut into wedges serve. Optionally serve dusted with powdered sugar.

Muriel's Steamed Christmas Pudding

This recipe was given to me by my former boss director of the Hotel Training school in Antigua Muriel O'Marde. This pudding was handed down from her mother recipe collection. Now it has become one of my favorite holiday desserts, and hope it will be one of yours too. This pudding is moist, rich and very tasty. I highly recommend it as a great dessert for your holiday guest can be paired with a light custard rum sauce. Best if made a day ahead before ready to serve.

Chef Freda

Servings: 12

About a month in advance soak ½ cup each of raisins, currants, sultanas, dried cranberries, candied cherries and mixed candied citrus peel in 2 cups of dark rum and 1 cup of cherry brandy (or other fruit-flavored liquor).

1 cup flour

1 tsp. ground cinnamon

1 tsp. ground allspice

½ tsp. ground nutmeg

1 cup liquid from the soaked fruits

1 cup fresh breadcrumbs made from day-old bread

½ cup butter, melted

1 cup packed brown sugar

2 large eggs

1 tbsp. grated orange zest

1 cup dark rum

Strain the liquid from the soak fruits and reserve 1 Cup of liquid.

In a large bowl mix together all the ingredients including the soaked dried fruits, rum and the 1 cup reserved liquid.

Pour mixture into an ovenproof pudding mold or bowl. Press mixture down slightly. Cover mold with a wax paper and tie with string to secure.

Place pudding in the bottom of the refrigerator to set ingredients (this step is optional).

Preheat the oven to 350° F (180° C).

Cover the pudding with a damp cloth and seal pudding with aluminum foil to prevent the cloth from burning.

Place the pudding in the oven in a large pan with hot water (water should come up half way to the bowl).

Reduce oven to 275° F (135° C). Steam the pudding for 2 - 4 hours.

Remove pudding from oven and cool before removing wrappings.

Lightly brush the pudding with 2 tbsp. of dark rum (optional).

Serve pudding with Rum Butter Sauce.

Rum Butter Sauce

1 cup powdered sugar

½ cup butter

¼ cup dark rum

Cream the butter and powdered sugar in a bowl. Beat in the rum slowly.

Chill sauce until ready to serve.

When ready to serve the pudding place on a large serving platter and serve with warmed rum butter sauce.

Optional: decorate the serving platter with mint leaves and cherries.

Christine's Chocolate Chunk & Coconut Mint Cookies

I created this recipe for my daughter Christine, her favorite cookies are chocolate chip, but I could not resist putting an island spin on these by adding some coconut and mint to the mix (sorry famous Amos). The result is a one of a kind cookie with an earthy tropical flavor and texture.

Chef Freda

Servings: 24 cookies

1 ¼ cup all-purpose flour

½ tsp. baking powder

¼ tsp. salt

1 stick butter, softened

½ cup brown sugar, firmly packed

¼ cup sugar

2 large eggs

1 tsp. vanilla extract

1 tsp. mint jelly

¼ cup grated coconut

¼ cup raisins

¼ cup semi-sweet chocolate chunks

Preheat the oven to 350° F (180° C).

Lightly grease 2 large cookie sheets.

Sift the flour, baking soda and salt in a bowl.

In a mixer cream the butter and sugars until the mixture is light and fluffy. Add the eggs one at a time, beating after each one is added. Add the vanilla extract and the mint jelly. Mix the mixture well.

Fold in the flour mixture, coconut, raisins and chocolate chunks.

Use an ice cream scoop to form the mixture into balls and drop onto prepared cookie sheets, leaving an inch of space between each cookie. Bake for 7 - 10 minutes.

Soursop Cheese Cake

Cheesecake, even though widely served in the Caribbean, is not a traditional Caribbean specialty. As a cheesecake lover I could not resist including a cheesecake recipe. In this recipe for sour cheesecake, I used a basic New York cheesecake base and added the tropical Caribbean flavor of the soursop.

Servings: 8 – 10

1 cup crushed vanilla wafers

4 tbsp. melted butter

1 ½ lb. cream cheese, softened

1 cup sugar

4 large eggs

1 ½ cups Soursop puree

4 tbsp. flour

1 tsp. vanilla extract

zest of 1 lemon, grated

Preheat the oven to 375° F (190° C).

Combine the vanilla wafer and the butter. Press the mixture evenly into a 10" spring form pan. Set aside.

In a mixer beat together the cream cheese and sugar until fluffy. Add the eggs one at a time, beating until mixture is fully combined. Add the soursop puree, flour, vanilla extract and lemon zest. Lightly beat the mixture until all the ingredients are combined. Pour the batter into the prepared pan.

Bake for 1 hour.

BAKING TIP

When making cheesecakes I normally bake in a water bath. I wrap the cheesecake in aluminum foil and place in a hot water bath and then bake. 15 minutes before finishing the baking I remove the cake from the oven, remove the foil and drain the water. I return cheesecake to brown. I found out that the cheesecake has a more creamy texture when using this method.

Remove cheesecake from the oven and cool to room temperature. Refrigerate for about 1 hour before serving.

To serve remove the cheesecake from the pan and place on a serving platter. Optionally serve with a berry or fruit sauce on the side.

Easy Coconut Cookies (Kid Friendly)

These easy coconut cookies are a fun and great way to get the kids in the kitchen. They are easy to prepare and the rich tropical coconut aroma will please any crowd.

Servings: 24 cookies

1 stick butter (½ cup)

¾ cup sugar

¼ cup coconut milk

⅔ cup shredded coconut flakes

1 ½ cups all-purpose flour

1 tsp. baking powder

1 tsp. vanilla extract

FROSTING

¼ cup confectioners' sugar (powdered sugar)

2 tbsp. coconut milk

½ cup coconut flakes

Preheat the oven to 350° F (180° C).

In a mixer, or by hand, cream the butter and sugar together until light and fluffy. Beat in the coconut milk and coconut flakes.

Stir in the flour, baking and vanilla extract.

Drop dough by the tablespoon onto a lightly greased cookie sheet.

Bake for 10 – 12 minutes, or until golden.

Let cool on the baking sheet for 3 minutes and then transfer to a wire rack to cool completely.

To frost the cookies sift the confectioners' sugar into a medium bowl. Add the coconut milk and mix until smooth.

Spread over the top of the cookies and sprinkle with the coconut flakes. Optionally the coconut flakes can be toasted in the oven before sprinkling on top of cookies.

Let cookies stand for 1 hour, or until frosting sets.

Serve or store in an airtight container.

Pastries, Pies & Puddings

Pumpkin Caramel Pudding

½ cup sugar

1 ½ lb. of pumpkin

2 pints of water

1 pinch of salt

2 tbsp. butter

½ cup all-purpose flour

2 cups evaporated milk

½ cup brown sugar

½ cup sugar

4 eggs, lightly beaten

1 tsp. vanilla extract

1 tsp. allspice

1 tsp. ground nutmeg mace

1 tsp. ground ginger

Make the caramel by placing the sugar in a small saucepan over medium heat and cooking until the caramel turns an amber color.

Pour caramel into a square pudding pan and swirl to cover the bottom of the pan.

Cut the pumpkin in small pieces, add to a pot of salted water, bring to the boil and cook until the pumpkin is tender. Remove pumpkin from the water, drain and remove the skin. Mash pumpkin with a fork until smooth.

In a large bowl combine pumpkin, butter, flour, milk, sugars, eggs, vanilla extract and spices. Mix all ingredients together until combined. Pour mixture into the prepared pan. Place pan in a larger pan that is a ¼ filled with hot water.

Bake the pudding in the oven for 1 ½ to 2 hours.

Remove pudding from oven and release the sides by running a knife around the edges.

Cool and unmold onto a serving platter.

Serve with cream.

Banana Bread Pudding with Caramel Butter Sauce

3 large ripe bananas, peeled and cut into chunks

¼ cup fresh lemon juice

½ cup light brown sugar

1 day-old medium loaf of bread, cut into cubes

¼ cup butter, melted

1 tsp. banana extract

1 tsp. ground nutmeg

1 tsp. ground cinnamon

¼ cup coconut rum

1 cup heavy cream or milk

2 large eggs

Preheat the oven to 350° F (180° C).

Lightly butter a 2-quart baking pan.

In a large mixing bowl lightly toss the bananas with the lemon juice, sugars and bread cubes. Leave for a few minutes.

In a separate bowl mix the butter, extract, spices, rum, cream and eggs until combined. Add to the bread mixture and combine together. Pour mixture into prepared pan.

Bake in the oven for 45 minutes. Turn oven down to 300° F (150° C) and bake for another 30 minutes.

Remove pudding from oven and cool.

Place on serving tray and serve with caramel butter sauce.

Caramel Butter Sauce

½ cup heavy cream

4 tbsp. butter

1 tsp. vanilla extract

2 tbsp. light corn syrup

¾ cup sugar

2 tbsp. water

In a small saucepan combine the heavy cream, butter and vanilla extract. Bring to a simmer and remove from heat.

In a heavy saucepan cook the syrup and sugar over medium heat until it reaches a light amber color. Adjust the heat and rotate pan to prevent burning as necessary.

Remove the caramel from the heat and add the cream. Be careful not to get burnt by the steam.

Return the pan to the heat and cook slowly, stirring until all the hardened sugar is dissolved and the caramel is bubbly.

Let the mixture cool and then whisk in the water.

Serve with banana bread pudding.

Sweet Potato Pudding

2 ½ cups milk

2 ½ cups sugar

1 egg

½ tsp. salt

1 tbsp. fresh ginger, grated

½ tsp. nutmeg

1 ½ tsp. cinnamon

4 cups sweet potato, grated

1 ½ cups coconut, grated

¼ cup flour

¼ cup raisins (optional)

Preheat the oven to 350° F (180° C).

Place all ingredients in a large bowl and mix together until fully combined. Pour into a lightly greased square baking pan or a casserole dish.

Bake in the oven for 45 minutes to 1 hour.

Remove from the oven and glaze with a simple syrup of sugar and water.

Cut into squares and serve warm.

Mango Pie

Servings: two 9" pies

pastry for 2 baked pie crusts (recipe follows)

3 cups peeled and sliced mangoes

½ cup sugar

2 tbsp. flour

2 tbsp. lemon juice

½ tsp. cinnamon

½ tsp. grated nutmeg

¼ cup raisins

1 tbsp. butter

Preheat the oven to 350° F (180° C).

In a large bowl combine mangoes, sugar, flour, lemon juice, cinnamon, nutmeg and raisins. Pour mixture into pie shell.

Decorate the top with a lattice of strips of pastry and dot with small pieces of the butter.

Bake for 1 hour.

Remove from oven and cool.

Serve warm.

PIE CRUST

1 ¼ cup vegetable shortening

3 cups all-purpose flour

1 egg beaten

5 tbsp. cold water

1 tsp. salt

Cut the shortening into the flour using the fingertips or a pastry cutter until it resembles coarse meal.

Mix egg with water in a small bowl, add to the flour mixture and blend well. Do not over mix.

Wrap dough in plastic wrap and chill for 5-10 minutes or until ready to use.

Did you know: The French islands of the Caribbean namely Martinique, Guadeloupe, Saint Marie and Saint Galant are famous for their French-inspired dishes. Being colonies of the French government, they have incorporated lots of French influences which are blended with the tropical ingredients grown on the islands resulting in tropical creole style cuisine.

Eat honey, my son, for it is good;
honey from the comb is sweet to your taste.
Know also that wisdom is sweet to your soul,
If you find it, there is a future hope for you,
and your hope will not be cut off.

Proverbs 24: 13-14

Mini Guava Tartlets

1 recipe for Sweet Pastry Dough (Basic Pastries section)

250 g guava paste

½ tsp. nutmeg

GUAVA PULP

3 ripe medium guavas, halved

1 cup water

½ cup sugar

1 stick cinnamon

Add the guavas, sugar and cinnamon to the water and cook until the guavas are soft. Remove the guavas from the liquid and place in a fine strainer. Use the back of a spoon to press the guavas through the strainer to get all the pulp. Set aside the pulp.

Preheat the oven to 350° F (180° C).

Turn the dough (Sweet Pastry Dough) out onto a floured surface and roll out about ⅛" thick. Using a 12 count muffin tin, cut out circles from the dough and press the dough down into each muffin tins compartment; you can also use mini tartlet tins. Cut out small strips from the remaining dough.

Mix the guava paste with the guava pulp (lightly heat guava paste to soften) until combined. Add the nutmeg and mix together. Spoon about 1 tbsp. of guava paste mixture into each muffin compartment (or 1 tsp. if you're using the small tart tins). Make sure you distribute the guava paste mixture evenly across the compartments/tins.

Decorate the tops with the dough strips in a crisscross. Be careful to seal and trim the edges.

Place the tins on a cookie sheet and bake for about 20 - 25 minutes, or until golden brown.

Leave the tartlets to cool before turning out onto a serving dish.

Dust them with powdered sugar.

Mango and Cream Cheese Turnovers

1 lb. frozen puff pastry (thawed and cut into 4 inch squares)

ground cinnamon, nutmeg, and cloves to taste

1 tbsp. butter

1 cup ripe mango, chopped

2 tbsp. brown sugar

1 tsp. ground cinnamon

1 tsp. ground ginger

¼ tsp. ground cloves

1/4 cream cheese softened

1 egg, beaten

confectioners' sugar for dusting baked turnovers

butter to grease the cookie sheet or line with a sheet of parchment paper

Grease a cookie sheet and line with parchment paper.

In a small saucepan over medium heat melt the butter. Add the chopped mangoes, sugar, cinnamon, ginger and cloves and cook until softened and combined. Set aside.

Sprinkle each pastry square with ground cinnamon, nutmeg and cloves to taste

Lightly spread the cream cheese mixture on top of each of the pastry squares. Put 1 ½ tbsp. of mango mix in the middle of each pastry square.

Brush the edges of the pastry with the beaten egg. Fold over to form a triangle and enclosing the mango mix.

Place the pastries about 2 inches apart on the prepared cookie sheet. Pick a hole in the top of each turnover to allow the steam to escape. Refrigerate for 20 minutes.

Preheat oven to 350° F (180° C).

Place the cookie sheet with the turnovers in the preheated oven and bake for 25 to 30 minutes, or until lightly golden. Remove from the oven.

Dust with confectioners' sugar.

Allow to cool before serving.

Bakewell Tarts

This is one of my all-time favorite English Tarts made with a filling of raspberry jam, topped with a nutty ground almond paste and a rich, sweet pastry crust. No picnic basket should be without a few of these.

CRUST

1 ¼ cups plain flour

¼ cup almond meal (ground almonds)

2 tbsp. sugar

1 stick (4oz) butter, chilled and diced

1 egg yolk,

1 tbsp. chilled water

¼ cup raspberry or cherry jam

¼ cup flaked almonds

FILLING

1 stick (4oz) of butter, softened

1 cup sugar

1 tbsp. lemon zest, finely grated

3 eggs

1 ½ cups almond meal (ground almonds)

⅓ cup all-purpose flour

Combine flour, almond meal, sugar and butter in a processor. Process until the mixture resembles fine breadcrumbs. Add egg yolk and 1 tbsp. chilled water. Process until dough just comes together, adding more chilled water if necessary. Turn the pastry out onto a lightly floured surface.

Knead until just smooth. Shape into a disc and cover with plastic wrap. Refrigerate for 30 minutes.

Preheat oven to 250° F (120° C). Adjust the heat if necessary.

Grease a 1" x 9" (approx.) deep loose-based, fluted tart pan. A regular tart pan can also be used.

Roll out pastry between 2 sheets of baking paper to just under ¼" thick (about 5mm). Line pan with pastry and trim excess. Refrigerate for 10 minutes.

Place the pan on a baking tray. Line the pastry case with baking paper and fill with dry beans, uncooked rice or baking beans. Blind bake for 10 to 12 minutes, or until the edges are lightly golden. Remove beans, or rice, and paper. Bake for another 7 to 8 minutes, or until the base is lightly golden. Set aside to cool. When the pastry case has cooled spread with jam.

Reduce oven to 250° F (120° C).

Meanwhile make filling: use an electric mixer to beat butter, sugar and lemon zest until light and fluffy. Add eggs, one at a time, beating until just combined. Beat in almond meal and flour.

Spread filling over the jam in the pastry case. Sprinkle with almonds.

Bake for 45 minutes or until a skewer inserted in the center comes out clean.

Cool slightly.

Serve warm with whipped cream.

Optional: dust with powdered sugar.

Baked Mango Crepes with Rum

Servings: 12 crepes.

CREPES

½ cup all-purpose flour

½ cup water

¼ cup milk

2 large eggs

1 ½ tbsp. unsalted butter, melted and cooled

½ tsp. sugar

pinch of salt

melted butter for cooking the crepes or cooking spray

MANGO FILLING

1 tbsp. butter, melted

3 large firm ripe mangoes, thinly sliced

2 tbsp. fresh lime or lemon juice

2 tbsp. sugar

½ tsp. ground cinnamon

⅓ cup dark rum

confectioners' sugar for dusting

In a medium bowl or mixer blend together the flour, water, milk, eggs, butter, sugar and salt for 1 minute, making sure not to over mix and that the mixture is fully combined.

Cover the bowl with a plastic wrap and let stand for 1 hour.

Heat a small to medium non-stick frying pan over high heat. Brush lightly with the melted butter or spray lightly with cooking spray. Be careful that it's not too hot or smoking.

Pour in about ¼ cup batter, tilt and rotate the pan to make sure that the batter covers the bottom and sides of the pan in a thin layer. Pour any excess batter back into the bowl.

Return the pan back to the heat and cook while loosening the edges with a metal spatula. Cook the crepe until the bottom is lightly brown and turn over and finish cooking until lightly brown. Remove the crepe and transfer to a plate.

Continue cooking the rest of the batter in the same way. Brushing the pan with butter as needed.

TO ASSEMBLE CREPES

Preheat the oven to 375° F (190° C).

Fold the crepes into quarters and place them on a baking sheet.

Brush the tops of the crepes with butter and bake in the oven for 10 minutes, or until lightly brown and slightly crisp.

In a small bowl, toss together the mango, lemon juice, sugar, cinnamon and rum.

Stuff the crepes with the mango mixture.

Place crepes on individual serving plates or a large platter.

Dust with the confectioners' sugar and serve warm.

French Islands Breadfruit Pudding

Do you know? Breadfruit was brought to the Caribbean by Lt. William Bligh and Captain James Cook who brought the breadfruit plant from Tahiti to the islands of Jamaica and St Vincent in late 1700's. The early British and French settlers had to find ways of feeding their growing colonies in the Caribbean. Breadfruit is widely used in the islands and can be prepared, boiled, fried, roasted or baked, as In this recipe for French Island Breadfruit Pudding.

2 cups breadfruit peeled, cooked and mashed

½ cup butter, melted

½ cup sugar

1 tbsp. flour

1 tsp. lime zest, grated

2 cups heavy cream

2 large eggs, lightly beaten

2 tsp. vanilla extract

1 tsp. ground nutmeg

1 tsp. ground cinnamon

Preheat the oven to 350° F (180° C).

Butter a medium baking dish or lightly spray with non-stick cooking spray.

In a large bowl, mix all the ingredients together until smooth. Pour mixture into the prepared baking pan.

Bake in the oven for 1 hour, or until knife inserted in the center comes out clean. Remove from oven.

Serve pudding warm.

Tropical Fruit Pizza

CRUST

2 cups all-purpose flour

½ tsp. baking soda

¼ tsp. salt

⅛ tsp. ground cinnamon

⅔ cup granulated sugar

⅔ cup brown sugar, unpacked

¼ cup unsalted butter, melted

2 large egg whites

¼ cup coconut milk

2 tsp. vanilla extract

¼ cup coffee (dilute 3 tbsp. instant coffee in ¼ cup warm water)

TOPPING

8 oz. cream cheese (⅓ less fat), softened

¾ cup powdered sugar

¼ cup coconut milk

1 tsp. vanilla

TO ASSEMBLE

1 large mango, diced

½ pineapple, cut into thin wedges

1 cup ripe papaya, sliced

1 cup star fruit, sliced

1 cup bananas, sliced (squeeze lime juice over bananas to prevent browning)

Preheat oven to 350° F (180° C).

Lightly spray a 9" x 13" x 1 ⅓" non-stick baking pan with cooking spray.

In a large bowl, combine the flour, baking soda, salt and cinnamon and stir to blend.

In another bowl, whisk the sugars together with the butter, egg whites, coconut milk and vanilla until light and fluffy.

Fold the dry ingredients into the wet ingredients with a spatula, in two additions, until the batter is well blended. Fold in the coffee mixture. Spread the batter onto the baking pan using the back of a measuring cup to smooth evenly.

Bake for 14 to 16 minutes, or until the edges are golden and a toothpick inserted into the middle comes out clean. Don't over-bake or the bars will be dry. Leave to cool completely on wire rack.

Meanwhile, prepare the topping: in a large bowl use an electric mixer to beat the cream cheese, powdered sugar, coconut milk and vanilla until well blended.

Cut the bars into 15 large squares (5 cuts by 3 cuts with the knife). Then cut each square in half diagonally to create triangles.

Spread the topping in a thin, even layer over the surface of the cookie, leaving a small margin around the edges.

Layer the fresh fruit over the frosting.

Store in the refrigerator until ready to serve.

Antigua Black Pineapple Pie

Antigua is known for its black pineapple; it is much smaller in size than its Hawaiian counterpart but much sweeter with a stronger color and flavor.

Servings: 6 - 8

2 prepared unbaked pie crusts

2 small Antigua black pineapples, peeled, cored & cut into small chunks

½ cup sugar

2 eggs

¼ cup flour

½ tsp. grated nutmeg

½ tsp. ground cinnamon

1 tsp. freshly grated ginger

1 tsp. vanilla extract

3 tbsp. butter melted

1 egg, lightly beaten for brushing

Preheat oven to 350° F (180° C).

Place one of the pie crusts in a greased pie pan and using a fork prick some holes in the bottom of the shell for steam to escape. Set aside.

In a medium bowl, beat the eggs and sugar until light and fluffy. Beat in the flour, spices and vanilla. Add the pineapple and melted butter and mix until fully combined. Pour mixture into prepared pie shell. Brush the edges of the pie shell with egg.

Cover the top of the pie with the other pie shell and press edges together with a fork to seal. Make some small holes in the top of the pie with the fork for the steam to escape. Brush remaining egg on the top of the pie.

Bake in the oven for 30 minutes, or until golden. Remove and cool.

Serve warm.

Caribbean Lobster Quiche

In our house, we enjoy making quiches, and I have experimented with lots of local island fillings, from, spinach, crab meat, chicken, ham, pumpkin, breadfruit, plantains, in this recipe using local lobster meat, the finished quiche makes an elegant addition to any lunch party or picnic.

Servings: 12

PASTRY (can be made night before)

2 cups all-purpose flour plus extra for dusting

1 tsp. salt

¼ tsp. sugar

¾ cup (1 ½ sticks) butter, diced

1 large egg yolk

3-4 tbsp. ice cold water

LOBSTER FILLING

3 tbsp. butter

2 medium green onions, chopped

2 sprigs fresh thyme, chopped

1 tbsp. curry powder

1 tsp. lemon or lime juice

1 lb. freshly cooked lobster meat, diced

1 ripe tomato, seeded and diced

salt and pepper to taste

6 large eggs

1 cup heavy cream

1 cup milk

1 cup shredded assorted cheese (cheddar, Swiss, provolone, parmesan)

TO MAKE THE PASTRY

In a large bowl, combine the flour, salt and sugar. Add the butter and mix with a pastry blender or fingers until mixture resembles coarse meal.

In a small bowl, combine the egg yolk with the water and add to the flour mixture. Mix lightly together until mixture forms a dough, but not sticky.

Wrap dough in a plastic wrap and chill in the refrigerator until ready to use.

TO MAKE THE FILLING

Melt the butter in a thick bottomed saucepan over medium heat. Add green onions, thyme and curry powder and cook for 3 minutes.

Add the lime juice, lobster meat, tomatoes, salt and pepper and stir to combine. Cook for 1 minute. Set Aside.

In a large bowl, mix the eggs until frothy. Add the cream and milk, season with salt and pepper and mix lightly together to combine.

Remove the dough from the refrigerator. Dust the rolling pin with flour and roll out the dough on a lightly floured surface.

Carefully roll the dough over the rolling pin and place over a lightly greased pie pan to cover. Press the bottom and edges firmly into the pan so that the pastry fits tightly. Trim the excess pastry from the rim of the pan and save for another use.

Place prepared pan on a sturdy cookie sheet this makes it easy to move around.

Place the lobster mixture in the bottom of the pan and spread evenly. Pour in the egg mixture and sprinkle the cheese mixture evenly over the top.

Bake the quiche in the oven preheated oven to 350° F (180° C) for 45 minutes to I hour, or until the quiche is set, puffy and not wet in the center.

Remove quiche from the oven and cool.

Loosen the quiche lightly from the pan, cut into wedges and serve.

Mrs. Barnes Easter Coconut Plate Tart

Mrs. Barnes was our neighbor in Antigua, and she was from the Island of Montserrat, Every Easter, it was always a treat when she brought over her Easter coconut plate Tart. I never got her original recipe. However, I created my own version of this deliciousness.

Chef Freda

Servings: 6 - 8

3 medium eggs

½ cup sugar

1 cup grated fresh coconut

1 cup coconut milk

½ cup evaporated milk

½ tsp. almond extract

zest of 1 lime, grated

1 tbsp. butter, melted

3 prepared pie crusts

1 egg, lightly beaten

Preheat the oven to 375° F (190°C).

Line a greased pie pan with one of the pie crusts. Prick the bottom to allow the steam to escape. Set aside.

In a mixing bowl beat the eggs and sugar until light.

Add the coconut, coconut milk, evaporated milk, almond extract, lime zest and melted butter. Mix thoroughly until mixture is combined.

Pour mixture into prepared pie shell. Brush the edge with the beaten egg. Use a knife to cut the remaining pie crust into medium strips and place in a crisscross fashion on top of the pie, pressing the edges to secure the strips.

Cut a medium ribbon strip a bit bigger than the top strips and form a ribbon around the edge of the crust. Use a fork to press the edges to secure. Brush with the remaining egg.

Bake in the oven for 20 - 30 minutes, or until set.

Remove from oven and cool.

Serve warm.

Cuban Style Guava Cream Cheese Tart

Servings: 8 - 10

CRUST

sweet pastry dough recipe for 2 crusts (Sweet Pastry Dough in Basic Recipes section)

FILLING

2 (8 oz.) packages cream cheese

2 lb. poached guava shells (or use 18 oz. can guava shells), drained well

1 tbsp. rum

1 ¼ cup brown sugar

2 cups of water

Preheat the oven to 350° F (180° C).

If using fresh guavas remove the seeds from the shell. Place the shells in a saucepan with the rum, sugar and water and bring to a boil over medium heat. Cook until guava shells are soft but not mushy. Remove from heat and drain.

Roll out the dough and line a lightly greased tart pan.

To make the filling cut the cream cheese into chunks and evenly distribute in the bottom of the tart pan.

Arrange the guava shells on the top of the cream cheese, cut sides down.

Roll the remaining dough and cut into strips. Cover the filling with the pastry strips in a lattice design.

Bake the tart for 35 - 40 minutes, or until golden brown.

Cool tart before removing from pan.

Serve sliced in wedges.

Coconut Cream Pie

Servings: 6 - 8

1 baked and cooled pie shell (Sweet Pastry Dough in Basic Recipes page)

⅔ cup sugar

¼ cup cornstarch

¼ tsp. salt

2 cups canned milk

3 large egg yolks, lightly beaten

⅔ cup coconut cream (Coco Lopez)

⅔ cup grated coconut

1 tsp. vanilla extracts

2 tsp. dark rum

1 tbsp. butter

Preheat the oven to 350° F (180° C).

In a medium pot combine the sugar, cornstarch and salt. Place over medium heat and gradually stir in the milk. Bring to the boil, stirring to prevent sticking. Reduce the heat to low.

Remove ½ cup of the mixture and gradually add it to the egg yolks, stirring to combine. Return the mixture to the pot, add the coconut cream and continue cook for another 2 - 3 minutes, or until mixture thickens.

Remove from heat and add the coconut, vanilla, rum and butter and stir to combine. Pour into the baked pie shell.

Top with meringue and bake for about 15 minutes, or until the meringue is golden brown.

Remove pie from oven and place on a wire rack to cool.

MERINGUE

3 egg whites

¼ cup sugar

⅓ cup shredded coconut

In a medium bowl beat egg whites until stiff peaks form. Fold in sugar and coconut. Spread on top of pie and bake.

Breadfruit Meringue Pie

I love lemon meringue pie and found that breadfruit, along with a nice mixture of spices, makes a unique tropical combination with a delightful blend of flavors that celebrates some great Caribbean ingredients.

2 eggs

1 pie shell

1 cup of flour

⅔ cup sugar

1 tsp. of salt

1 tsp. of salt

1/4 cup of raisins

1/4 cup dried cranberries or currants

2 tsp. vanilla

2 cups coconut milk

½ tsp. nutmeg

½ tsp. baking powder

2 cups grated breadfruit (uncooked)

Directions: Preheat oven to 375° F (190° C).

Mix together all of the ingredients until smooth.

Pour into a 9" pie shell.

Bake in a hot oven for 50 minutes to 1 hour.

Remove from the oven and top breadfruit filling with meringue (recipe below).

Return to the oven for at least 10 minutes, or until meringue is set.

Serve warm or chilled.

MERINGUE

2 egg whites

6 tbsp. granulated sugar

Beat the egg whites until peaks form. Add sugar and continue beating until stiff peaks form.

Cornmeal Coconut Pudding

This cornmeal pudding is pretty old school. It was a local favorite at our bakery and is quick and easy to make. It's sure to be a crowd pleaser. Just keep the drinks flowing as it can sometimes have a dry texture.

Servings: 12

2 cans coconut milk

1 lb. yellow cornmeal

1 cup grated coconut

1 cup sugar

2 medium eggs

1 tsp. vanilla extract

¼ cup raisins

½ cup flour

1 tsp. ground cinnamon

3 cups water

Preheat the oven to 350° F (180° C).

Combine all the ingredients in a large mixing bowl and use a whisk to mix together. Pour mixed ingredients into a greased cake pan.

Bake for 30-45 minutes.

While still in the oven, check to see if the pudding is done by shaking the pan to see if the top is set. If the middle appears to be still liquid bake for a few more minutes. You can also check for doneness by inserting a skewer in the center. Pudding is done when the skewer comes out clean.

Remove pudding from the oven and cool.

Cut into squares and serve with custard or whipped cream.

Caribbean Old Fashioned Bread Pudding

5 loaves day-old bread, broken into pieces and soaked in water

1 ½ cups brown sugar

1 cup white sugar

4 large eggs

2 sticks butter or margarine, melted

2 cups evaporated milk

2 cups raisins

1 tsp. cinnamon

1 tsp. grated nutmeg

1 tsp. almond extract

Preheat oven to 350° F (180° C).

Prepare 8 small round ramekins by spraying with a non-stick spray and dusting lightly with flour.

Squeeze excess water out from soaked bread by pressing through a sieve. Place bread in a bowl and add sugars, margarine, milk, eggs and mix until combined.

Add the raisins and spices followed by the nutmeg, cinnamon and almond extract.

Place portions of batter in prepared ramekins and bake for 35 minutes, or until golden.

Serve with Coconut Custard (recipe below).

Coconut Custard

1 cup coconut milk

½ cup sweetened condensed milk

2 tbsp. sugar

1 tbsp. rum

zest of 1 lime, grated

1 tbsp. cornstarch mixed with 1 tbsp. water

In a small saucepan bring the coconut milk, condensed milk, sugar, rum and grated lime zest to a boil. Reduce to simmer and simmer for 5 - 10 minutes until sugar is dissolved and the mixture is combined.

Lower heat and add the cornstarch mixture. Cook, stirring constantly, until the mixture has thickened slightly. Remove from heat.

Serve warm.

Puerto Rico Coconut Bread Pudding

1 can (13.5 oz.) unsweetened coconut milk

2 cups milk

½ cup half-and-half

1 (1 lb.) French bread loaf, cut into 1" cubes (do not remove crusts)

3 large eggs

¾ cup granulated sugar

1 ½ tsp. vanilla extract

½ cup plus 2 tbsp. firmly packed sweetened coconut flakes

⅓ cup golden raisins

1 tbsp. butter

3 or 4 ripe mangos, peeled and sliced (optional)

Mix together coconut milk and half-and-half in a large mixing bowl. Fold the bread into the liquid, making sure all the bread cubes are moistened. Allow the bread to soak while you beat together the eggs, sugar and vanilla extract in a small mixing bowl. Add egg mixture to the soaked bread. Stir in 1/2 cup of the coconut flakes and the raisins.

Grease a 13 x 9-inch baking pan with 1 tbsp. butter.

Spoon the batter into the pan and sprinkle the remaining 2 tbsp. coconut flakes on top.

Bake on the upper rack of a preheated 350° F (180° C) oven until the bread pudding has set and is golden brown on top, about 45 minutes.

Cut the bread pudding into squares.

You can serve the pudding hot, warm or chilled; on its own or with mango slices.

Spanish Meat Pie

This meat pie is made from a mixture of beef and pork. It is made on some of the Spanish-speaking Caribbean Islands where some of the ingredients are sometimes substituted to suit the cook's preferences. Corn meal is sometimes added when making the dough on some of the Islands. The mixture can also be made into beef patties or empanadas. This can be served as a light lunch with salad or is great for company gathering. It is usually better served as a left over when the flavors had time to mingle better together.

Caribbean Spanish Meat Pie

1 lb. ground meat (beef, pork, chicken, turkey)

1 tbsp. olive oil

¼ cup salt pork (I use pancetta) or bacon, cubed

½ cup smoked cured ham, cubed

2 garlic cloves, minced

2 tbsp. green peppers, seeded and chopped

1 small jalapeno pepper, seeded and chopped (use plastic gloves)

1 medium onion, peeled and chopped

1 tsp. oregano

1 tsp. fresh thyme

¼ tsp. vinegar

6 dried pitted plums (prunes), chopped

1 medium tomato, chopped

2 tbsp. raisins

6 Spanish pitted green olives, chopped

2 tsp. capers

1 can (12 oz.) crushed tomatoes

salt to taste

Brown pancetta in a medium skillet, drain excess fat remove from pan and reserve.

Add ham to skillet and brown. Set aside.

Drain fat from skillet and return to medium heat. Add olive oil and ground meat and brown stir mix with a spoon to prevent meat from clumping. Reduce heat and add other ingredients including pancetta and ham. Cover and cook over medium heat for 10 - 15 minutes, stirring occasionally. Remove the lid and cook for another 10 minutes.

Adjust the seasoning if needed.

Remove from heat and cool.

DOUGH

2 cups flour

4 tsp. baking powder

1¼ tsp. salt

½ cup shortening

¾ cup cold water

Pre-heat the oven to 350° F (180° C).

Sift together flour, baking powder and salt. Cut shortening into flour, with fingertips or pastry blender, until mixture looks like coarse corn meal.

Add milk gradually, stirring until flour is moistened. Turn dough onto a floured board, shape into a ball and divide dough in half.

Roll out ½ the dough on a lightly floured rolling pin into a circle to fit a 9-inch greased pie pan.

Roll dough over rolling pin and unroll over the pie pan. Do not stretch the dough. Prick bottom and sides of dough in several places to allow air to escape.

Filled lined pie pan with meat filling.

Proceed with other half of dough in the same way and cover the filling with it. Prick top of dough in several places. Join edges of dough together by pressing them together with a finger or a fork.

Brush top lightly with milk to give a golden glaze.

Bake the pie at 350° F (180° C) for 30 minutes.

Increase heat to 375° F (190° C) and bake for a further 10 - 15 minutes.

Remove from oven, cool and serve.

Amouy's Sweet Potato Pie

This is my daughter Amouy's favorite pie which she enjoys serving during the holidays. Here she uses cooked and mashed sweet potato or yams: the bright yellow variety. However, I have also used the local Caribbean potato and have gotten great results. Because Caribbean potatoes are a bit more starchy and dryer, it's best to add more milk or cream to the mixture.

Chef Freda

Servings: 8

2 cups cooked, mashed sweet potatoes (or 16-oz can sweet potatoes drained, mashed and passed through a sieve to remove lumps)

½ cup firmly packed brown sugar

½ tsp. salt

½ tsp. ground cinnamon

½ tsp. ground nutmeg

¼ tsp. ground allspice

1 cup light cream or canned milk

3 eggs lightly beaten

1 unbaked pie shell (recipe in the Basic Recipes section)

Preheat the oven to 350° F (180° C).

In a large bowl combine the sweet potatoes, sugar, salt, cinnamon, nutmeg and allspice. Add the egg and cream and mix together until fully combined and the mixture is smooth. Pour the filling into the pie shell.

Bake the pie in the pre-heated oven for 15 minutes.

Reduce the heat to 325° F (160° C) and bake for a further 35 - 40 minutes, or until the filling is set.

Remove the pie from the oven and cool.

Caribbean Street Food and Snacks

Antiguan Beef Patties

½ lb. short crust pastry

3 tbsp. vegetable oil

1 lb. ground beef

1 onion, finely chopped

2 green onions, finely chopped

2 garlic cloves, minced

½ red bell pepper, finely chopped

2 sprigs fresh thyme leaves, finely chopped

1 tsp. hot sauce

2 tbsp. fresh breadcrumbs made from day-old bread

salt to taste

2 eggs, lightly beaten for brushing

Preheat the oven to 350° F (180° C).

Over medium heat in a medium-sized skillet, heat oil and brown the ground beef. Remove from heat and drain any excess fat.

Add onion, green onion and garlic and cook for 5 minutes. Add the bell pepper, thyme, hot sauce and bread crumbs and season with salt and pepper, to taste. Stir to combine.

Roll out the pastry on a floured surface. With a round cookie cutter or large glass cut the pastry into circles.

Put 2 - 3 tbsp. mixture onto one half of the dough circle. Brush the edges with the egg mixture, fold in half and seal the edges with a fork.

Place on a greased cookie sheet. Use a fork to make a few small holes in the top of the patties for the steam to escape. Brush the patties with the egg mixture.

Place in the oven and bake for 20 - 30 minutes.

Chicken Quesadillas

3 boneless, skinless chicken breasts

2 tbsp. Taco Seasoning

vegetable or olive oil for frying

1 large onion, chopped

½ large green bell pepper, chopped

½ large red bell pepper, chopped

12 small flour or whole-wheat tortillas

2 cups cheddar-jack cheese, grated

½ cup hot sauce

butter for frying salsa

sour cream for serving

cilantro, chopped for garnish (optional)

jalapeno, sliced for garnish (optional)

Heat the vegetable or olive oil in a skillet over high heat.

Sprinkle both sides of the chicken with taco seasoning. Add the chicken to the skillet and sauté over medium-high heat until done, about 4 minutes per side. Remove from the skillet and cool slightly. Cut into cubes and set aside.

In the same skillet over medium-high heat, sauté the onions and peppers until the veggies are golden brown, 3 to 4 minutes. Remove and set aside.

Melt ½ tbsp. of butter in a separate skillet or griddle over medium heat. Lay a flour tortilla in the skillet. Build the quesadillas by adding a generous amount of grated cheese to the tortilla. Then add the chicken and cooked peppers on the cheese. Drizzle over some hot sauce and top with a little more grated cheese. Top with a second tortilla.

When the tortilla is golden on the underside carefully flip the quesadilla to the other side: add ½ tbsp. butter to the skillet at the same time. Continue cooking until the second side is golden.

Repeat with the remaining tortillas and fillings.

Cut into wedges and serve with salsa, sour cream, jalapeno slices and cilantro.

Spanish Shrimp Empanadas (Pastelitos)

FILLING

1 lb. medium shrimp, cleaned, peeled, and tails removed

¼ cup white onion, finely diced

2 cloves garlic, minced

1 large red bell pepper, roasted and sliced into thin strips

pinch of chipotle or cayenne pepper

salt and freshly cracked pepper

juice of ½ a lemon or lime

olive oil

handful of chopped cilantro

In a medium bowl combine the shrimp with chipotle, or cayenne pepper, salt, fresh cracked pepper, lemon juice and about 2 tbsp. of olive oil. Set aside.

In a large saute pan heat 2 tbsp. of olive oil over medium-high heat. Add the onions and cook for 3 to 4 minutes. Add the garlic and cook for a further minute. Add the shrimp and cook just until shrimp turns pink, 3 to 4 minutes. Add the roasted red pepper and stir well to combine.

Adjust the seasoning with salt if desired. Remove from heat and cover.

MASA HARINA CORN DOUGH

2 cups masa harina (found in the most Hispanic grocery stores)

1½ cups warm water

1 tbsp. chicken bouillon powder

1 tbsp. chili ancho powder or any mild chili powder

1 tbsp. granulated garlic

1 tsp. salt

2 tbsp. canola oil plus more for frying

Combine all of the dry ingredients in a bowl and gradually add the warm water while working the masa dough with your hands. Once all the water has been mixed in add 2 tbsp. of oil and work into the masa.

Make 12 masa balls, cover with plastic wrap and set aside.

Heat about 2 cups of canola oil to medium heat in a heavy, shallow pan.

While the oil is heating up you can start to assemble the empanadas. Line a tortilla press with a heavy plastic storage bag, cut to size to fit the tortilla press. Leaving the bottom of the bag intact cut the other three sides open.

Line a plate with paper towels and set aside.

Use the tortilla maker and press one dough ball, about 4 to 4½ inches across. Make sure you don't press it too thin. Fill with 2 tbsp. of shrimp filling and about 3 sprigs of cilantro. Pick the empanada up with the plastic and fold to close. Use your fingers to seal, folding the edges gently. Carefully pull the plastic away from the empanada.

Transfer empanada to the hot oil and cook for about a minute on each side, or until crispy. Drain on a plate lined with paper towels.

You can keep them warm on a baking sheet in the oven pre-heated to 250° F (120° C) while you finish frying the rest of the empanadas.

Serve right away or cool completely before storing in an airtight container.

To reheat the empanadas place them in a 400° F (200° C) oven for 20 minutes.

Jamaican Patties

Jamaican patties are an all-time favorite Caribbean snack! They are embraced all over the world with fillings like chicken, beef, vegetable, lobster and fish blended with the tropical seasonings and spices of the islands. Jamaicans and other islanders universally embrace them. This will make a great holiday snack to keep and to share. In this recipe I used chicken. However, the filling can be adjusted to suit your taste.

Servings: 6 large patties or 12 small

PASTRY

2 cups all-purpose flour

1 tbsp. ground turmeric or annatto

1 tsp. salt

1 stick (½ cup) butter

¾ cup cold water

Sift the flour, turmeric and salt in a bowl. Cut the butter into small pieces and add to the flour mixture. Mix well with fingers until the mixture resembles coarse meal or breadcrumbs.

Wrap dough in plastic and chill for 45 minutes to 1 hour

FILLING

2 tbsp. butter or margarine

1 medium onion, finely chopped

2 large cloves garlic, finely chopped

1 hot pepper, deseeded and chopped (or use 2 tsp. hot sauce)

2 sprigs thyme, finely chopped

2 sprigs fresh chives, finely chopped

2 sprigs fresh parsley, finely chopped

2 large tomatoes, finely chopped

2 large boneless chicken breasts cut into small cubes to make 2 cups (or use ground beef, fish or mixed vegetables)

1 tsp. ground turmeric or annatto

1 tsp. ground ginger

½ tsp. ground cumin

1 tsp. allspice

¼ cup chicken stock

salt and pepper to taste

1 tbsp. brandy or rum

Heat the butter in a large saucepan. Cook the onion, garlic, hot pepper, thyme, chives, parsley and tomatoes until softened. Add the chicken and the remaining spices and stir to combine. Season with salt to taste.

Add the stock and cook over medium heat for 15 minutes, or until liquid has evaporated. Add the brandy and stir to combine. Remove from heat and cool.

GLAZE

2 egg yolks, beaten together in a small bowl

Preheat the oven to 400° F (200° C).

Roll out the pastry and cut into circles using a small saucer (about 8 – 12").

Place 2 tbsp. of the filling on one half of the circle, brush the edge lightly with the egg yolk and fold the other side over so that the edges meet. Crimp edges together using a fork until edges are sealed.

Place the patties on a greased baking sheet and brush tops with the beaten egg yolks.

Bake the patties for 35 minutes, or until tops are golden. Serve hot.

Grilled or Baked Plantains

I had the pleasure of enjoying these at a Road Side Barbecue in Roseau Dominica. They were worth the wait in line as I patiently waited behind the local taxi men and bystanders to get my early morning grilled plantain fix. I have prepared them at home in the oven using both my oven and charcoal grill. For the best flavor use plantains that are ripe but still firm (half ripe).

Servings: 4

4 large half ripe plantains

2 tbsp. melted butter (optional)

Peel and remove skin. Place plantain on a platter and brush with butter.

Grill over hot coals or in the oven until done and golden.

Don't worry if you get some crispy areas, this gives it a more intense roast flavor.

Titiri Ackra (Mini Fish Fritters)

Growing up in the village of Marigot on the north-eastern side of the island of Dominica, I remember enjoying the delightful taste of Titiri Accra (Fritters) made from the small, seasonal river fish found in the local rivers.

2 lbs. fresh titiri, washed and drained to remove excess water

2 cloves garlic, chopped

2 sprigs fresh thyme, chopped

2 hot peppers, chopped

1 tsp. freshly squeezed lemon juice

2 tsp. salt

1 ½ cups all-purpose flour

oil for frying

Into a large bowl add the Titiri, garlic, thyme, peppers, lime juice, salt and flour.

Mix together until all ingredients are combined. Heat the oil in a large saucepan or deep fryer.

Drop mixture by the medium-spoonful into the hot fat and cook, turning, until brown on all sides (do not over crowd the pan).

Drain on a platter lined with paper towel.

Serve hot with more hot sauce, if desired, and lime wedges.

Banana Fritters

This is still one of my family favorites that's quick and easy to make and is a great way to use up very ripe bananas.

3 ripe Bananas (I use those that are very ripe with dark speckled skin)

1 tsp. vanilla extract

2 tbsp. granulated sugar

1 ½ tsp. baking powder

⅓ cup milk

1 medium egg (optional)

8 - 10 tbsp. flour

½ tsp. ground cinnamon

½ tsp. grated nutmeg

Mash the bananas.

In a medium bowl, combine flour, baking powder, sugar, cinnamon and nutmeg. Add milk, egg, vanilla and bananas and mix to combine.

Heat up enough oil in a cast iron frying pan, or pan of choice, to deep fry.

Dip a large spoon into oil and then scoop up a spoonful of batter and drop into the hot oil.

Deep fry the fritters until they are brown and crisp on the edges.

Drain on paper towels.

Serve warm.

Salt Fish and Bake

SALT FISH

1 lb. salted cod or other salted fish

8 cups water for boiling, or as needed

TO PREPARE SALT FISH

Add salt fish and 4 cups of water to a large saucepan and bring to a boil. Boil for 10 to 15 minutes. This can also be done overnight. I prefer to soak the salt fish for a few hours before cooking to remove excess salt. After the fish has boiled for 15 minutes drain water and replace with another 4 cups of fresh water. Bring to a boil and boil for another 15 minutes.

Once the fish has boiled for another 15 minutes remove from water and let cool. When fish has cooled flake with a fork or your hands until all the flesh is completely flaked.

TO MAKE SALT FISH FILLING

3 tbsp. vegetable oil or butter

2 large tomatoes, diced

½ cup mixed bell peppers (red, yellow, green), finely chopped

5 green onions, finely chopped

3 cloves garlic, finely chopped

1 tbsp. dried thyme

pinch of cayenne pepper

Heat the oil in a large saute pan on medium heat. When the oil is hot add tomatoes, green onions, bell peppers and garlic. Cook until tomatoes are soft. Add the prepared flaked salt fish, thyme and cayenne pepper. Cook for 10 to 15 minutes, occasionally stirring to ensure even cooking. Once the fish has cooked for 15 minutes, remove from the heat.

BAKES

3 cups flour (plus ¼ cup for kneading)

1 cup sugar

2 tsp. baking powder

1 ½ cups water

4 cups canola or vegetable oil for frying

TO MAKE BAKES

In a large mixing bowl add flour, sugar, baking powder and mix together thoroughly. You can use a whisk for this step or use your hands. Make a well (hole) in the center of the mixed dry ingredients. Add water and knead to form soft dough. Continue kneading until the dough is smooth. Cover with a damp paper towel and leave to rest for at least 30 minutes.

After the dough has rested roll into a log on a floured surface and cut into 9 pieces. Knead each piece into a smooth ball. Cover with a damp paper towel and rest for another 15 to 30 minutes.

When the dough is ready for frying heat 4 cups of oil in a pot large enough for deep frying. The oil should be about 300° F (150° C). If you bring it up to 350° F (180° C), the regular temperature for deep frying, the bakes will burn and the inside will be raw. Adjust the heat during the frying process as necessary.

Roll each dough ball into a flat disk and submerge in the oil. The dough will initially sink to the bottom of the pot and then it will rise to the surface and begin to swell. After about 2 minutes, or when the underside of the bake is brown, flip the bake over to brown the top side. When both sides of the bake are browned remove from oil and place on a dish lined with paper towels.

Fish Taco's

1 lb. firm white fish, such as tilapia, snapper, cod, mahi or catfish

2 medium limes, halved

1 clove garlic, finely chopped

¼ tsp. ground cumin

¼ tsp. chili powder

2 tbsp. vegetable oil plus more for oiling the grill grates

kosher salt and freshly ground black pepper to taste

½ small green or red cabbage (about 14 oz.), cored and thinly sliced

½ medium red onion, thinly sliced

¼ cup fresh cilantro, coarsely chopped

6 - 8 soft 6" corn tortillas

Optional Garnishes:

sliced avocado

guacamole

salsa

sour cream

hot sauce

Fish tacos can be filled with either fried or grilled fish.

Place the fish in a baking dish and squeeze half a lime over it. Add the garlic, cumin, chili powder and 1 tbsp. of the oil. Season with salt and pepper to taste. Turn the fish in the marinade until evenly coated. Refrigerate to marinate at least 15 minutes.

Make the slaw and warm the tortillas while the fish is marinating

Combine the cabbage, onion and cilantro in a large bowl and squeeze half a lime over it. Drizzle with the remaining 1 tbsp. oil, season with salt and pepper and toss to combine. Taste and add more salt and pepper if necessary. Set aside.

Warm the tortillas by heating a medium frying pan over medium-high heat. Add 1 tortilla at a time, flipping to warm both sides, for about 5 minutes in total. Wrap the warm tortillas in a clean dishcloth to keep warm and set aside while you prepare the fish.

Brush the grates of a grill pan or outdoor grill with oil and heat over medium-high heat. Remove the fish from the marinade and place on the grill. Cook the fish for about 3 minutes (without moving the fish). It should have grill marks and is white and opaque on the underside. Flip and grill the other side until white and opaque, about 2 to 3 minutes more. (It's OK if it breaks apart while you're flipping.) Transfer the fish to a plate.

Taste the slaw again and season as needed with more lime juice.

Slice the remaining lime halves into wedges and serve with the tacos.

To construct a taco, break up some of the cooked fish and place it in a warm tortilla. Top it with slaw and any optional garnishes.

Beef and Cheddar Pinwheels

DOUGH

1 cup milk

¼ cup brown sugar

¼ cup shortening

1 egg

1 packet fast active/rapid rising yeast (about 1 tbsp.)

3 cups flour

1 tsp. salt

1 egg white

FILLING

1 lb. lean ground beef

½ large onion, finely chopped

4 cloves garlic, finely chopped

1 tsp. brown sugar

1 tbsp. soy sauce

1 tsp. dried thyme

1 tsp. spicy brown mustard (or substitute with yellow mustard and a dash of hot sauce)

salt and pepper to taste

1 tsp. oil

4 tbsp. ketchup

9 tbsp. ketchup for garnish

½ lb. cheddar cheese, shredded

TO MAKE THE DOUGH

Warm the milk and add sugar and egg. Whisk together.

Add wet ingredients to a large mixing bowl or stand mixer with a dough hook. Sieve the flour into a separate mixing bowl. Add yeast and salt to flour and mix together.

Add dry ingredients, 1 cup at a time, to wet ingredients and mix together to form soft dough. Place dough on a floured surface and knead together to form a smooth ball.

Grease a large mixing bowl with about 2 tbsp. oil. Place dough in greased bowl. Turn dough to coat with oil from the bowl. Cover dough and leave until it doubles in size, about an hour.

TO MAKE THE FILLING

Combine beef, onion, garlic, brown sugar, soy sauce, thyme, mustard, salt and pepper in a large mixing bowl. Mix together and leave to marinate for about 30 minutes.

Add oil to a large skillet on medium heat. When the oil is hot add marinated ground (minced) beef. Cook until beef fully cooked through. Stir constantly to ensure even cooking, about 10 mins.

Stir in 4 tbsp. ketchup, remove from heat and let cool.

TO MAKE THE PINWHEELS

Preheat oven to 375° F (190° C).

Once the dough has doubled in size remove from bowl. Punch down dough on a floured surface. Use a rolling pin to roll the dough to about ½" thickness.

Spread cooked and cooled beef evenly over the dough. Add ¾ of the shredded cheese. Roll dough into a log. Seal ends by pinching them together. Brush log with egg white. Cut into ½" pieces. Top with swirls of ketchup and then the remaining shredded cheese. Let it rest for about 30 minutes.

Bake for 20 to 35 minutes at 375° F (190° C).

Pine (Pineapple) Tarts

Servings: about 12

3 cups crushed pineapple

1 cup granulated sugar

1 tsp. cinnamon powder

1 egg yolk, beaten

1 recipe for Short Crust Pastry (recipe next page)

Preheat oven to 350° F (180° C).

Combine all the ingredients in a small saucepan and cook on medium heat until the pineapple juice reduces to a jam-like paste. Set aside and let cool.

To shape the pine tarts: separate the pastry dough into 10 or 12 pieces. Roll each piece on a floured surface until the dough is the thickness of a coin. Use a circular mold to cut the rolled dough into circles.

Fill the circle with a heaped tablespoon of pineapple filling and shape into a triangle. Seal the ends with a fork.

Place on a baking sheet lined with parchment paper.

Brush with egg yolk.

Bake the tarts for 20 to 25 minutes.

Short Crust Pastry Dough

(Makes 1lb. pastry dough)

4 cups flour

1 cup vegetable shortening

1 stick (¼ cup) butter

about 8 tbsp. ice cold water

Rub or cut shortening and butter into flour until mixture forms a breadcrumb-like texture.

Add ice water, 1 tbsp. at a time, and pinch mixture together to form soft dough. Do not knead.

Separate mixture into two and chill in the refrigerator for at least 1 hour.

Use pastry for pineapple tarts

Currants Roll

DOUGH

3 cups flour

8 tbsp. butter, chilled and diced

½ cup vegetable shortening, chilled and diced

¼ tsp. salt

1 cup iced water, or more as needed

FILLING

1 ½ cup dried currants or raisins (or mixture of both)

¼ cup brown sugar

1 tbsp. ground cinnamon

½ tsp. ground nutmeg

½ cup butter, melted

1 egg, beaten in 1 tbsp. milk

1 tbsp. vanilla extract

sugar for sprinkling

Cut the cold butter and vegetable shortening into pieces.

Sift the flour into a food processor bowl and add salt, butter and shortening. Give the mixture a few pulses in the food processor until the mixture has the size of peas. This can also be done in a large mixing bowl using your fingers to lightly incorporate the butter and shortening into the flour. Be careful not to over mix.

Add ¾ cup of water to start and then gradually add the remaining water until the dough takes shape.

Place the dough on a flour-dusted surface and work quickly to form a smooth ball of dough. Cover with plastic wrap and place in refrigerator to cool and firm up, about 2 hours.

In a large bowl place the cinnamon, nutmeg, currants and/or raisins and brown sugar and mix together. Add and mix in the vanilla.

Remove dough from refrigerator. Cut the dough into 2 pieces.

Roll one piece of dough on a floured surface to a rectangular shape that is less than ¼" thick.

Brush the surface with half the melted butter.

Evenly distribute half of the currants mixture on the dough, leaving a 1" border from the edge with no filling.

Roll the dough very tightly into a cigar-like cylindrical shape. The tighter it is the more layers you're the currants roll will have. Pinch the ends to seal.

Repeat with the other piece of dough and the remaining currants mixture.

Place the rolls on a baking sheet lined with parchment paper or lightly greased and lightly dusted with flour.

Beat the egg and milk together and brush the surface of each roll. This will give them a nice golden color when baked.

Sprinkle with a little sugar (optional) and place the baking sheet in the middle of the oven pre-heated to 350° F (180° C) for about 50 minutes.

Brush with melted butter and sprinkle with sugar immediately after removing from the oven for a final special touch.

Allow to cool before slicing. The traditional way is to cut diagonally.

St. Lucia Baked & Stuffed Breadfruit

2 tbsp. butter

2 stalks chives, chopped

1 medium onion, chopped

1 clove garlic, finely chopped

½ lb. ground beef or ground turkey

½ lb. chopped ham

1 tomato, chopped

1 whole breadfruit

1 tbsp. butter, melted for basting pepper

salt to taste

Pre-heat the oven to 350° F (180° C).

Parboil the breadfruit in salted water.

In a medium saucepan melt the butter. Add chives, onion and garlic and saute lightly. Add ground beef and ham and cook until beef is no longer pink, about 10 minutes. Add tomato, pepper, and salt set aside.

Peel and core breadfruit and fill with the meat mixture. Brush breadfruit lightly with butter and place in a greased casserole dish.

Bake in a preheated oven for about 30 minutes, basting during baking.

Remove from oven and rest for a few minutes before slicing into portions.

Serve warm.

Cuban Sandwiches (Cubanos)

Servings: 4

1 Cuban bread loaf

3 tbsp. butter

1 tbsp. yellow mustard (optional)

2 tbsp. fresh mayonnaise (optional)

1 lb. ham

1 lb. Cuban pork or roast pork

½ lb. Swiss cheese

15 slices dill pickles

Preheat a large cast iron skillet or a large grill fry pan to medium hot.

Cut the bread into sections of about 8 inches long. Cut these in half and with spread with butter on the inside and outside of both halves.

Mix together the mustard and mayonnaise.

Make each Cuban Sandwich (Cubano) with the ingredients in this order: pickles, roast pork, a light spread of the mustard mixture, ham and cheese. Top with the other half of bread.

Place the sandwich in the skillet or pan and weigh down with a heavy pan or pot. Press down firmly and cook for about 3 minutes per side or until golden brown and the cheese has melted.

Remove from pan and rest for a minute before cutting in half and serving.

Sausage Rolls

1 ½ lb. good quality link sausage (beef, pork, turkey)

1 tsp. dried basil

1 tsp. dried oregano

1 tsp. dried thyme

salt and freshly ground pepper, to taste

1 Recipe Quick Puff Pastry (recipe in Basic Recipes section)

2 eggs, beaten

Preheat the oven to 375° F (190° C).

In a large bowl, mix together the sausage, basil, oregano, thyme, salt and pepper. Mix until all the seasonings are well distributed throughout.

Roll out all the puff pastry into one large rectangle about ⅛" thick. Put the wide side of the rectangle to your left.

Form the sausage meat into a log about 1" thick and long enough to fit the width of the pastry. Lay this log along the whole edge. Roll the pastry around the sausage, brush with beaten eggs at the join. Trim the pastry so that it overlaps slightly. Repeat the process with the remaining sausage meat and pastry.

Place the sausage rolls about 1" apart on a baking sheet making sure the seam is at the bottom. Brush the tops with beaten egg and cut the sausage rolls into either 1 ½" or 3" logs.

Bake for 15 to 20 minutes, or until golden brown and the meat is cooked.

You can also freeze the uncooked rolls to be baked later.

Serve warm or cold.

Coconut Cake Tarts

Coconut Cake Tarts are found in most bakeries on the island of Antigua. Using fresh coconut for the filling will give you the best results.

Servings: 6 - 8 tarts

PASTRY

2 ½ cups all-purpose flour

1 ½ tsp. baking powder

½ tsp. salt

1 tsp. ground cinnamon

¾ cup vegetable shortening or margarine

1 ½ cup brown sugar

¼ cup water

1 tsp. vanilla extract

In a large bowl sift together the flour, baking powder, salt and cinnamon.

Add the shortening and lightly blend into the flour mixture with a pastry blender, or fingertips, until the mixture resembles coarse meal. Set aside.

In a smaller bowl add the sugar, water and vanilla extract and mix together to combine and make light syrup.

Gradually add the syrup into the flour mixture, a little at a time, and mix into a smooth dough that's not sticky.

Remove dough and dust lightly with flour. Cover and set aside.

COCONUT FILLING

3 cups freshly grated coconut

1 ½ cups brown sugar

1 tsp. cinnamon

1 tsp. ground nutmeg

1 tsp. vanilla extract

2 tbsp. water plus extra to moisten pastry edges

In a medium bowl place all ingredients and mix together until fully combined. The filling can also be cooked. If cooked cool completely before using.

Preheat the oven to 350° F (180° C).

Flour a flat surface and roll out the pastry with a flour-dusted rolling pin roll to about ½" thick.

Use a large round pastry cutter, or a saucer, to cut the pastry into round discs. Place a mound of coconut filling on one half of the circle and moisten the edge with some water. Fold the other half over the filling and seal the edge of the pastry. You use your finger or a fork to seal the edge together.

Place tarts on a lightly greased cookie sheet. Prick some holes on the top of the tarts with a fork for the steam to escape.

Bake in the oven until golden.

Trinidad's Shark and Bake

Servings: 8

FOR THE BAKE

2 cups all-purpose flour

3 tsp. baking powder

1 tsp. salt

1 ¼ stick butter (about 10 tbsp.)

1 tsp. sugar

¾ cup water or more if needed

vegetable oil for frying

In a large bowl, sift the flour, baking powder and salt together.

Add the butter and with fingers, or a pastry cutter, mix butter into the flour mixture.

Add the sugar and combine into the flour mixture.

Gradually add the water until smooth dough is formed.

Cut the dough into 6 pieces and form into balls.

Let the balls stand for a few minutes to relax the dough balls.

Press the balls into 1" thick round discs.

Heat the oil in a heavy bottomed large pot or a deep fryer over medium.

Add the bakes and fry on both sides until golden, occasionally turning for even browning and cooking on both sides.

Remove bakes from the oil and place on a paper towel-lined plate to drain.

FOR THE SHARK

6 shark steaks

2 cloves garlic, chopped

1 medium onion, finely chopped

1 small hot pepper, chopped

juice of 1 lime or lemon

In a shallow dish add the shark steaks, garlic, onion, pepper and lime juice and marinade for 1 - 2 hours. You can also marinate overnight.

Remove shark steaks and run under cold water.

Set aside to drain.

HERB SEASONING MIXTURE

3 cloves garlic, finely chopped

3 sprigs thyme, finely chopped

3 sprigs of chives, finely chopped

1 hot pepper, deseeded and finely chopped

1 tsp. salt or to taste

In a small bowl mix all the ingredients together.

SEASONED FLOUR

¾ cup flour

salt and pepper to taste

½ tsp. curry powder

Place the flour onto a flat plate, add the salt, pepper and curry powder and mix together.

Sprinkle the seasoning mixture on both sides of the shark steaks.

Dip both sides of the steaks into the flour mixture.

Fry the steaks in the vegetable oil for about 10 minutes, turning to cook both sides thoroughly.

Remove steaks from the oil and drain on paper towels.

SHADOW BENNIE (CILANTRO) SAUCE

¾ cup Shadow Bennie, washed and finely chopped

2 cups white vinegar

4 cloves garlic, finely chopped

3 tsp. vegetable or olive oil

1 small hot pepper, deseeded and finely chopped

¾ cup freshly squeezed lime or lemon juice

½ cup parsley, finely chopped

2 tsp. thyme, finely chopped

In a medium bowl, mix all ingredients together and place in a tightly covered jar or dish until ready to use. This can be made in advance or overnight.

TO ASSEMBLE

Cut the bakes horizontally open through the middle.

Place the shake steak in the middle and top with Shadow Bennie Sauce.

Repeat with remaining bakes.

Serve warm with hot sauce.

Dominica Patty Coco

This is a special treat on the island of Dominica. It is similar to the cake tart found in Antigua, but with less sugary dough.

Servings: 6 - 8 tarts

DOUGH

2 cups all-purpose flour

½ tsp. baking powder

2 tbsp. sugar

½ tsp. salt

¼ cup vegetable shortening

¼ cup water

In a large bowl, sift together the flour, baking powder, sugar and salt.

Add the shortening and blend together without over mixing.

Add the water, a little at a time, and form into smooth dough. Do not over mixing.

Dust lightly with flour cover and set aside.

COCONUT FILLING

2 cups freshly grated coconut

1 cup brown sugar

1 tsp. cinnamon

1 tsp. ground nutmeg

1 tsp. vanilla extract

½ tbsp. water plus extra to moisten pastry edges

In a medium bowl, place all ingredients and mix together until fully combined. The filling can also be cooked. If cooked, cool completely before using.

Preheat the oven to 350° F (180° C).

On a floured surface with a flour-dusted rolling pin, roll out the pastry to about ¼" thick.

Use a large round pastry cutter, or a saucer, to cut pastry into round discs.

Place a mound of coconut filling on one half of the circle and moisten the edges with some water. Fold the other half over the filling and seal the edge of the pastry. You can use your finger or a fork to seal the edge together.

Place tarts on a lightly greased cookie sheet. Prick some holes in the top of the tarts with a fork for the steam to escape.

Bake in the oven until golden.

Basic Recipes

Quick Puff Pastry

4 cups all-purpose flour

1 ½ tsp. salt

6 ½ sticks (3 ¼ cups) unsalted butter, chilled and cut into ½" cubes

1 cup cold water

Sift together the flour and salt into the bowl of a food processor fitted with the blade attachment.

Add chilled, diced butter and pulse three to five times, or until the butter pieces are about the size of Lima beans. Add water to the mixture and pulse again for about three times. Invert the crumbly pastry mixture onto a lightly floured work surface.

Use a rolling pin and bench scraper to shape the pastry mixture into a long rectangle. Use the bench scraper to carefully flip one-third of the rectangle towards the center. Then flip the other end to the center (like folding a business letter). Rotate the dough 90 degrees.

Reshape and roll the dough into a rectangle. Repeat the folding and rotating process three more times, for a total of four turns. If the dough becomes soft or sticky during this process, immediately refrigerate until firm again. Wrap the dough in plastic wrap. Refrigerate the dough at least 45 minutes, or until firm.

TIP: make four indentations in the dough, one for each time the dough has been turned, with a finger. This way you can keep track of how many times the dough has been turned.

After the dough has been refrigerated for 45 minutes, unwrap and discard the plastic.

Keep your work surface and rolling pin well-floured.

Press down on each of the four sides of dough to seal its shape.

Start with the rolling pin at the center. Roll away from you. Return to the center and roll towards you. Repeat the folding and rotating process of the dough two more times for a total of six times.

After the sixth turn, wrap the finished dough in plastic wrap and refrigerate to make ensure it is well chilled before using.

Quick Puff Pastry keeps for up to three days refrigerated or frozen for several months.

Sweet Pastry Dough

12 tbsp. (6 oz.) unsalted butter at room temperature, plus a little for pans

¼ tsp. sea salt

1 cup plus 1 tbsp. confectioners' sugar, sifted

⅓ cup plus 1 tbsp. almond flour, sifted

1½ tsp. vanilla extract

1 extra-large egg, beaten

1¾ cups plus 1 tbsp. cake flour, sifted

In a standing mixer fitted with paddle attachment, cream butter and salt on medium speed for 1 minute.

Scrape down sides of the bowl and continue mixing. Add confectioners' sugar and combine with butter, mixing at low speed.

Scrape down the bowl and mix again. Add almond flour and vanilla and mix at low speed until combined.

Gradually add egg and ½ cup cake flour. Beat at low speed until just incorporated.

Scrape down the bowl and mix again. Gradually add remaining cake flour and mix just until the dough comes together. Do not over beat. Dough should be soft to the touch.

Scrape dough out of the bowl and gently press into a ½" thick rectangle. Airtight double-wrap with plastic and refrigerate for at least 3 hours, preferably overnight.

Very lightly brush two tart pans with butter.

Cut dough into two equal pieces. Wrap one piece and refrigerate while you roll out the other half. Lightly dust parchment paper or a silicone baking mat with flour. Tap dough lightly with a rolling pin to make it more pliable.

Begin rolling gently, three times in one direction from the edge nearest to you to the far edge.

Rotate dough a quarter turn clockwise. If it's sticking, run an offset spatula underneath to loosen it, gently lift and lightly dust with flour underneath. Repeat the process until dough is about ¼" thick. Check often to make sure dough is not sticking, and dust with flour as necessary.

Cut dough into a 10 ½"circle. If it's on a silicone mat flip it over onto a piece of lightly flour-dusted parchment and peel off the mat. Very lightly dust dough with flour and brush away excess flour with a dry pastry brush.

Loosely roll dough onto rolling pin and then unroll it onto a tart pan, making sure to cover pan evenly. Gently ease it into the pan so that there is no gap between the bottom edge of the ring and the bottom of the pan; don't press hard or the dough will be thinner in places. Cut away excess dough by holding a paring knife perpendicular to the edge of the pan and turning the pan around against the edge of the knife.

Use a fork to poke little holes in dough over the entire bottom of the shell. Refrigerate dough, uncovered, for at least 1 hour and preferably overnight. If freezing the dough, refrigerate for 1 hour, then double-wrap in plastic wrap and then wrap in foil and freeze.

Repeat process of rolling out dough with the other dough half.

Heat the oven to 325° F (160° C). Place the rack in the middle of the oven.

Place tart pan on a baking sheet. Line shell with parchment paper and fill to the top with pie weights, dried beans or rice.

Bake for 15 minutes. Remove parchment and weights and return to oven for another 10 to 15 minutes, or until golden brown.

Remove from oven and cool completely on a wire rack; leave the pan on the baking sheet.

When cool add filling.

Basic short crust pastry Dough

1 cup all-purpose flour

½ tsp. kosher salt

1 stick unsalted butter, chilled and cut into □" pieces

3 tbsp. ice water

Put flour and salt in the bowl of a stand mixer or food processor.

Add butter and quickly cut it into flour until mixture resembles coarse meal. Add iced water and mix briefly, about 30 seconds to form soft dough.

Remove dough from bowl and shape into a thick disk. Wrap in plastic wrap and refrigerate for at least 2 hours, or overnight.

Bring to the dough to cool room temperature before rolling. Lightly flour dough and counter top. Roll out gradually, periodically letting the dough to rest for a moment before continuing. This makes rolling easier and will stop the dough from shrinking back during baking.

Roll dough into a thin round of approximately 13" in diameter. Trim to make a 12" circle. Refrigerate the trimmings for patching.

Lay dough loosely into a 9 ½" fluted tart pan with a removable bottom. Leave for a bit to allow the dough to relax.

Fold the overlap of the dough back inside to make a double thickness. Then press firmly against the pan so the finished edge is slightly higher than the pan.

Refrigerate or freeze for an hour before pre-baking.

Jellies, Jams, Preserves and Butters

Mango Butter

This rich tropical-flavored butter will be a great accompaniment to a crusty loaf of island yeast bread or any of the other sweet quick breads.

½ cup honey

¼ cup softened butter

¼ cup ripe mango, chopped

1 tsp. rum

In a medium bowl with a hand mixer, or spoon, whip all the ingredients together until combined.

Serve immediately or cover and store in the refrigerator.

Bring to room temperature when ready to use.

Pineapple Mint Butter

½ cup honey

¼ cup softened butter

¼ cup pineapple, chopped

1 tsp. fresh mint, finely chopped

1 tsp. coconut cream

In a medium bowl with a hand mixer, or spoon, whip all the ingredients together until combined.

Serve immediately or cover and store in the refrigerator.

Bring to room temperature when ready to use.

Guava Jelly

3 lb. of ripe guavas

3 cups sugar

1 cup of water

pinch of grated nutmeg

Process half of the guavas with half of the water in a blender until smooth.

Pour the mixture into a deep, non-reactive pot. Repeat the process with the rest of the guavas and the water.

Add the sugar and nutmeg and cook over medium heat, stirring regularly, for about 2 hours, or until big bubbles rise up.

While hot strain the mixture and discard the guava seeds.

Pour into jars.

Passion Fruit Jam

10 passion fruit

juice of ½ lemon

1 ½ cup sugar

Wash the passion fruits. Halve and scoop out the pulpy seeds. Set aside in the fridge.

Put half the quantity of the shells in a pot and fill with enough water to just cover the tops. Boil for about 30 - 40 minutes, or until they turn translucent and soft. Drain and cool for easier handling. Save 1 cup of boiled liquid.

When cooled, scoop out the inner flesh and discard the papery skins. Pulse the flesh in a food processor, or blender, until you have a smooth puree.

In a deep thick bottomed pot add the puree, the reserved seeds, lemon juice, reserved boiled liquid and sugar. Stir over medium heat until all the sugar has dissolved and then bring to a boil. Reduce the heat to low and let it simmer for 15 minutes, stirring lightly with a wooden spoon to prevent burning.

Turn off the heat and skim the scum from the jam surface with a spoon.

Leave to cool before ladling into clean, sterilized jars. Close the lid and leave the jars upside down for 10 minutes.

The jam will thicken up as it cools.

Store in the fridge.

Pineapple Ginger Jam

3 ½ cups sugar

2 (4-lb.) pineapples, peeled, cored and cut into ¼" thick rings and coarsely chopped (about 8 cups)

¼ cup fresh ginger root, peeled and finely chopped

1 tsp. lime juice

In a heavy kettle combine the sugar and 2 cups water. Bring the mixture to a boil, stirring until the sugar is dissolved. Boil the syrup until it reaches 220° F (105° C) on a candy thermometer. Alternatively drop a few drops into a small bowl of cold water. The mixture should form a soft ball.

Stir in the pineapple, ginger root and lime juice. Simmer the mixture uncovered, stirring to prevent scorching, for 1 hour, or until it registers 220° F (105° C) on a candy thermometer. Alternatively drop a few drops of the mixture into a small bowl with cold water. The mixture should form a soft ball.

Remove the kettle from the heat and ladle the preserves into 5 sterilized jars. Wipe the rims with a dampened towel and seal the jars with the lids.

Put the jars into a water bath canner, or on a rack set in a deep kettle, add enough hot water to the canner or kettle to cover 2" of the jars and bring to a boil. Cook the jars, covered, for 10 minutes. Use tongs to transfer the jars to a rack to cool completely.

Store the jars in a cool, dark place.

Banana Chutney

8 oz. currants

8oz raisins

1 ½ pt. (3 cups) malt vinegar

12 oz. brown sugar (about 2 ⅓ cups)

1 tsp. turmeric

1 tsp. curry powder

1 tsp. salt

1 tsp. ground ginger

1 lb. onion, finely chopped

10 green bananas, peeled and roughly chopped

Chop the currants and the raisins and soak them in vinegar overnight.

Add the sugar, turmeric, curry powder, salt, ginger, onions and bananas.

Place in a heavy bottomed pan and bring to a boil. Reduce heat to a simmer and cook for 25 - 30 minutes.

Store the chutney in an airtight container.

Serve warm.

Soothing the Soul: "A Spot of Tea"

Hibiscus Flower Lime Tea

½ cup dried hibiscus flowers

1 sprig fresh rosemary

1 tbsp. freshly squeezed lime or lemon juice

2 tbsp. honey or sweetener, to taste

6 cups of water

In a medium saucepan on medium heat, add the water, hibiscus flower and rosemary and bring to a boil.

Reduce the heat to a simmer, cover the pot loosely and simmer the mixture for 30 - 35 minutes.

Remove from the heat and add the lime juice.

Strain and add sweetener to taste.

Serve Hot.

St Lucian Cocoa Tea

3 oz. local Caribbean Chocolate, roughly chopped

1½ cup water

2 cups milk (I prefer canned milk)

2 fresh Christmas leaves or spice leaves

1 small piece mace (outer shell of the nutmeg)

2 sticks cinnamon

sugar to taste

In a medium saucepan over medium heat bring the chocolate and water to a boil.

Boil the chocolate mixture, stirring to break up the chocolate pieces, for about 5 minutes.

Add the milk, spice leaves, mace and cinnamon stick and reduce heat to a simmer.

Cook for another 10 -15 minutes, stirring occasionally.

Remove from heat and add sugar to taste.

Strain with a fine-mesh strainer.

Serve hot.

Pepper Mint Tea

3 sprigs fresh peppermint, washed thoroughly

1 cup boiling water

sugar or honey to taste

Add fresh peppermint to the water and bring to boil.

Remove from heat and leave for 2 - 3 minutes to steep.

Add sweetener to taste.

Fever Grass Tea

2 stalks fever grass, washed

1 cup boiling water

sugar or honey to taste

Steep the fever grass in hot water for 3 - 5 minutes.

Add sweetener to taste.

Serve hot.

Ginger Tea

1 small piece fresh ginger root, washed thoroughly, skinned and mashed

1 ½ cups water

½ tsp. lime juice

honey or sugar to taste

Add the ginger root to a small pot with water and bring to the boil.

Boil for 5 -10 minutes.

Remove from heat and add the lime juice. Strain the tea.

Add sweetener to taste.

Soursop Leaf Tea

3 Soursop leaves

1 ½ cups water

honey or sugar to taste

Add the soursop leaves to a small pot with water to the boil for 5 -10 minutes.

Remove from heat and cover. Steep the tea for 1 minute.

Add sweetener to taste.

Serve hot.

Lime Leaf Tea

4 fresh lime leaves, washed

1 ½ cups water

honey or sugar to taste

Add the lime leaves to a small pot with water to the boil for 5 -10 minutes.

Remove from heat and cover. Steep the tea for 5 - 10 minute.

Add sweetener to taste.

Serve hot.

Some Favorite Caribbean Spices

Cumin: this is a strong, warm and pungent spice used mostly in Caribbean Indian cooking. Cumin works well in puddings and cakes.

Turmeric: is made from the dried turmeric root, which is ground into a bright yellow spice. It has a peppery and earthy taste and is used in baking, mostly for its color.

Allspice: is widely used in making fruit cakes. It is a berry-shaped spice and when grounded gives off a light cinnamon clove aroma.

Nutmeg: is a must for most Caribbean bakers. This large, aromatic seed is grown on most of the islands, especially on the island of Grenada which is known as the spice island of the Caribbean. Nutmeg gives off a warm spicy flavor when used in cakes, breads and drinks. Nutmeg has a better flavor when freshly grated.

Cinnamon: this warm and spicy spice is available in stick and powder form. It is widely used in cakes, puddings, sweets, drinks and desserts.

Mace: mace is the outer casing of the nutmeg. It is a little milder than the nutmeg. Used in puddings, tea cakes and flavored butter.

Cloves: cloves are used either whole or powdered in baking cookies and cakes.

Star Anise: is a star-shaped spice and is used to flavor jellies and juices.

Fresh Ginger Root: fresh ginger is grown on most of the islands. The roots are washed, peeled and grated or sliced. It is widely used in making cakes, puddings, cookies and desserts.

Vanilla: vanilla pods are dried and the seeds removed after the pods are split open. The seeds are scraped out and added to cakes, pies, cookies and puddings. Vanilla extract made from distilled vanilla pods are more readily available and more widely used.

Yeast Tip

When using yeast for these recipes I prefer to use quick-rise yeast for some sweet bread recipes since the dough takes half of the time to rise. I also use active dry yeast when making some bread recipes. The yeast used should always be fresh. Always check the use-by date.

Cooking Measurement Equivalents

1 tbsp. (tbsp) =	3 tsp. (tsp)
1/16 cup =	1 tbsp.
1/8 cup =	2 tbsp.
1/6 cup =	2 tbsp. + 2 tsp.
1/4 cup =	4 tbsp.
1/3 cup =	5 tbsp. + 1 tsp.
3/8 cup =	6 tbsp.
1/2 cup =	8 tbsp.
2/3 cup =	10 tbsp. + 2 tsp.
3/4 cup =	12 tbsp.
1 cup =	48 tsp.
1 cup =	16 tbsp.
8 fluid ounces (fl oz) =	1 cup
1 pint (pt) =	2 cups
1 quart (qt) =	2 pints
4 cups =	1 quart
1 gallon (gal) =	4 quarts
16 ounces (oz) =	1 pound (lb)
1 milliliter (ml) =	1 cubic centimeter (cc)
1 inch (in) =	2.54 centimeters (cm)

Source: United States Dept. of Agriculture (USDA)

Notes about Measuring and Baking Equipment

It is very important to measure ingredients correctly when preparing a baking recipe. For most of my recipes I prefer to use stainless steel measuring cups and spoons for dry ingredients. For liquids I use glass measuring cups.

Dry Ingredients

When measuring dry ingredients keep in mind that flour, sugar, cornmeal and other dry ingredients might set during storage and you may need to stir them before measuring. Be sure not to press down, or pack, and to always level the top off with a spatula or pallet knife. With the exception of brown sugar which needs to be pressed and packed into the measuring container.

Flours

Most of the recipes in this book use all-purpose flour. However, there might be a few recipes that use for cake flour. Cake flour can be purchased separately; it's a lighter version and great for making delicate and lighter cakes, cupcakes and tea cakes. I also make my own by adding cornstarch to the flour to lighten it: 1 cup cornstarch to 2 cups flour.

Sugars

For most recipes that user sugar I use regular granulated sugar. For brown sugar I use light brown sugar and for dusting I use 10 times powdered sugar or icing sugar.

Yeast

I use active dry yeast for most bread recipes because they are mostly bought in bulks of 16 oz. or more. The readily available and quick yeast found in most food stores can also be used with good results. Carefully read the directions and also check the expiration dates to make sure that the yeast is still fresh enough to use.

Baking powders and baking soda

Be careful when using baking powder and baking soda. Using too much or too little can result in either a great end product or a terrible, inedible one. Be especially careful when using baking soda. Using too much can give your product a soapy taste. Also, I find baking soda works better when used in baking with other ingredients such as honey, buttermilk, sour cream, etc.

Nuts

I love cooking with nuts and find that they give great texture and flavor to baked goods. Be mindful that when using nuts you are aware of the people that will be eating your products. There are lots of people these days, especially children, who have nut allergies. Know before you serve.

Nuts are prone to grow rancid quickly, especially in tropical climates, so it's best to store them in a cool, dry place, before and after use. I personally find the best places to buy nuts are at a health food stores. Even though the price might be higher, the product tends to be of a better quality.

Dairy Products and Baking Fats

Shortening, Butters and other Fats

Most of the recipes in this book use shortening, butter and vegetable oil. Some local Caribbean bakeries use lard, which is a pork fat product. I prefer not to use pork fat as a personal preference. I use an organic shortening for most of my bread recipes, but you can use whatever you prefer. For a recipe using butter I use pure butter and not butter spreads as most butter spreads have a greater percentage of water which does not give you a good baking result. Margarine can be substituted. Keep in mind when using margarine that your product might be a bit heavier. When making cakes and using margarine beat a bit longer and add a small amount of fruit juice to lighten, if desired.

Eggs

Whenever I use eggs, especially in cakes, I remove them from the refrigerator and bring to room temperature before using. I find that I get better volume and cakes are lighter.

Dried Fruits

Before using dried fruits in cakes or breads plump them up a bit by placing in cold water and bringing to the boil. Drain and cool before using. As with most Caribbean bakers, I always keep dried fruit soaked in rum, brandy or cherry brandy liquid so it's always on hand when you need it. As I remember from our bakery, we soaked our dried fruits a year in advance before we needed them.

Tools and Equipment

Back in the days, we did all our bread making and cake mixing by hand. Now, most bakeries have mixers, food processors and all the necessary tools to make baking a snap. Still, there are ways to improvise if you do not have all the required baking equipment.

Mixers: I still sometimes use a hand mixer when beating eggs especially if I don't want to mess up a large stand-up mixer. This can also be used to mix batters.

Food processors: I love my food processors! They are great for chopping nuts, pureeing, grating and grinding and chopping. But I still find that my metal grater works best when I am grating coconuts.

Spatulas: works great for loosening baked goods from the sheet pan and for spreading frosting on cakes. The rubber spatulas are great for mixing, folding and spreading batters.

Bowls: are always useful in baking weather plastic or metal. They have a variety of uses.

Baking pans: come in all shapes and sizes. Most are very versatile and can be used for different needs.

I am the true vine, and my father is the gardener. He cuts off every branch in me that bears no fruit while every branch that does bear fruit, he prunes so that it will be even more fruitful

John 15 1-2

Author: Freda Gore

Email: **caribbeanculinarytours@gmail.com**

Made in the USA
Columbia, SC
22 November 2022